The Epistles of John and Jude
Personal Workbook

By Chad Sychtysz

© 2025 Spiritbuilding Publishers.
All rights reserved. No part of this book may be reproduced in any form without the written permission of the publisher.

Published by
Spiritbuilding Publishers
9700 Ferry Road, Waynesville, Ohio 45068

THE EPISTLES OF JOHN AND JUDE
Personal Workbook
By Chad Sychtysz

ISBN: 978-1-964-80545-0

Spiritbuilding
PUBLISHERS

spiritbuilding.com

Table of Contents

Introduction to 1 John 1
Prologue (1:1–4) 9
Lesson 1   Walking in the Light of God (1:5–10) 12
Lesson 2   The "New Commandment" to Love (2:1–14) 17
Lesson 3   The Promise of Eternal Life (2:15–29) 24
Lesson 4   Children of God and Children of the Devil (3:1–10) 32
Lesson 5   "Love One Another" (3:11–24) 37
Lesson 6   The Spirit of Truth and the Spirit of Error (4:1–6) 45
Lesson 7   "God Is Love" (4:7–21) 49
Lesson 8   Jesus Is the Christ, the Son of God (5:1–12) 55
Lesson 9   Praying with Confidence (5:13–21) 60
Introduction to 2 & 3 John 69
Lesson 10   The Epistle 2 John 72
               Salutation and Introduction (1:1–3) 72
               Walking in the Truth (1:4–6) 73
               Those Who Do Not Walk in Truth (1:7–11) 74
               Closing Remarks (1:12–13) 78
Lesson 11   The Epistle 3 John 81
               Salutation (1:1–2) 81
               Walking in the Truth (1:3–4) 81
               Accepting "Strangers" (1:5–8) 82
               Contrast of Two Men (1:9–12) 84
               Closing Remarks and Farewell (1:13–15) 88
Introduction to Jude 91
               Salutation (1:1–3) 96
Lesson 12   Condemnation of Ungodly Men (1:3–16) 98
Lesson 13   Prescription for Godly Living (1:17–25) 107
Sources Used for 1–2–3 John and Jude 114
Endnotes 116

Scripture taken from the NEW AMERICAN STANDARD BIBLE®,
Copyright © 1960, 1962, 1963, 1968, 1971, 1972, 1973, 1975, 1977, 1995 by
The Lockman Foundation. Used by permission.

The author of this workbook can be contacted at chad@booksbychad.com.
Cover design by Larissa Lynch

Introduction to *1 John*

The First Epistle of John (*1 John*) is one of the most intriguing and rewarding books of the New Testament (NT). Its language is simple and straightforward, making it easy to read; however, its "simple" prose belies a great complexity to the subjects, themes, and theological doctrines contained within. The epistle is densely packed with fundamental truths woven into a rich tapestry of practical Christian living. Its style is unique among NT writings; only the Gospel of John comes close to it.

While "John" was a common name in the ancient world, there is substantial agreement among the "church fathers" (early Christian writers and prominent figures), historians, and Bible scholars that the author of *1 John* is John the hand-picked apostle of Jesus. John was the son of Zebedee and brother of the apostle James (Mark 1:19). John and James, with their father, ran a fishing business in Galilee; they either employed Peter or he worked alongside them (Luke 5:10). John was an early disciple of John the Baptist and was with the prophet when he (John the Baptist) introduced him to Jesus (John 1:35ff). Later, Jesus appointed him to be one of His twelve disciples (Mat. 10:2). Along with his brother, James, and his friend and fellow co-worker, Peter, John enjoyed a privileged relationship with Jesus that was even closer to Him (in earthly friendship) than the rest of the twelve apostles.

John refers to himself anonymously as "the disciple whom Jesus loved" (John 13:23, 20:2, 21:7, and 21:20). This further indicates the close and special relationship that Jesus and John shared. This especially bears true in the fact that, while He was on the cross, Jesus entrusted the future care of His own mother, Mary, to John (John 19:26–27).

John and James were not as outspoken and impetuous as their fellow disciple Peter, yet clearly, they saw themselves as leaders of the group. This is most evident in their appeal (along with that of their mother, whose name is withheld in Scripture) to sit on either side of Jesus' throne when He began to reign in His kingdom (Mat. 20:20ff and Mark 10:35ff). This is a remarkable request and is not one we would expect of someone who was soft-spoken, reserved, and hiding in the shadow of an assertive man like Peter. There is only one instance where the gospels identify John alone as the speaker: when he wanted Jesus to silence a man who was casting out demons in His name (Mark 9:38 and Luke 9:49).

At the time that the church was established (in Acts 2), Peter served as the leading spokesman of "the twelve," but John was often close by his side. These two men represented the new movement before the Jewish Council (Sanhedrin); accordingly, they were the first to be arrested because of their prominent roles (Acts 4:1ff). John apparently remained in Jerusalem after the church was dispersed—a dispersion largely due to the persecution instigated by Saul (Acts 8:1–4), but he did go to Samaria with Peter to impart to the new Christians there the power of the Holy Spirit (to do miracles; Acts 8:14). After this, John slipped into obscurity, being eclipsed by Peter's ministry, a growing number of other church workers and leaders, and especially Saul (Paul) himself.

Tradition says that John, in later life, moved to Ephesus and continued to teach and minister into old age. Because of his leadership in the church, Emperor Domitian (ruled AD 81–96) exiled him to the remote island of Patmos for a time (Rev. 1:9).[1] (Patmos is a small island in the Aegean Sea, almost due west of Miletus in Asia Minor.) During this exile, John received his apocalyptic vision from Christ—later called *Revelation*. According to early church tradition, John outlived all his fellow apostles. Irenaeus wrote that John lived until the reign of the Roman emperor Trajan (ruled AD 98–117).[2] Tradition also says that John is the only apostle who died of natural causes, rather than facing martyrdom as his brother, James, did (Acts 12:1–2).[3]

No reputable scholar has questioned the authenticity of John's first epistle.[4] The writing style, word choices, and themes ("Word," light, love, truth, confidence, etc.) between John's gospel and *1 John*, indicate common authorship. Also, many early Christian writers quoted or attributed *1 John* to the apostle John.[5] Thus, every investigation into either the internal or external evidence concerning authorship easily leads to the same conclusion: whoever wrote the *Gospel of John* also wrote *1 John*. If it is not the apostle John, then we have no one else to consider seriously.

John did not personally identify himself to his readers, likely because they already knew who he was. He seems to have enjoyed a close relationship with them, having intimate knowledge of their successes (2:12–14), struggles (4:1–6), and need for encouragement (3:1–3, 5:13–15, etc.). His epistle is likely not addressed to any one church, but to a group of churches—possibly the seven churches of Asia, the same to which Jesus' revelation to John would be addressed (Rev. 1:10–11).[6] It is generally accepted that John wrote this epistle in the late first century, but scholars are divided on exactly when. Most agree that it was between AD 80 and 100, and particularly around 90–95. The absence of any references to the persecution of John's readers, especially due to emperor worship, is conspicuous. Since the persecution that plagued the seven churches in *Revelation* began in the mid-90s, John's epistle was likely written before it began—specifically, before his exile to Patmos.

Purpose of Writing: Most scholars and commentators agree that a main purpose for John's epistle is to combat a doctrinal heresy called Gnosticism that had found its way into the church. "Gnostic" is from the Greek word *gnosis*, translated "knowledge" in English-speaking Bibles.[7] Thus, Gnostics place a great deal of emphasis on knowledge as a means of drawing near to God rather than on love, service, good works, or holiness. Gnosticism is the humanly invented doctrine that *special* or *mystical* knowledge is the route to divine favor. It is an elitist view, since only certain people will have (or can obtain) this knowledge, while other (deemed *lesser valued*) Christians will not. It is also a "dualistic way of looking at God, humanity, and the world."[8]

Gnostics claimed they could obtain spiritual freedom *not* through the blood of Christ and Christian living, but by unlocking spiritual mysteries of the universe, allegedly given to them by God. This forced a *separation* between the physical or carnal world and the intellectual or spiritual one. In other words, if all one needs is knowledge, then pious living is unnecessary. Simon Kistemaker sums up Gnosticism with these basic points:

- The world is evil. This evil causes a separation, in the form of an unbridgeable gulf, between the world and the supreme God. Therefore, the supreme God cannot have created the world.
- The God of the Old Testament created the world. He is not the supreme God, but an inferior and evil power.
- Any teaching of the incarnation [i.e., God being made flesh; John 1:14] is unacceptable. It is impossible for the divine Word to live in an impure [human] body.
- There can be no resurrection of the body. They who are set free experience liberation from the shackles of an impure body.[9]

Gnosticism attempted to resolve an age-old problem that has bothered men for millennia, namely, how a *good God* could have created a *sinful world*. Biblical teaching reveals that the responsibility for sin lies with the people whom God created, not the God who created people, but Gnostics sought a more esoteric and satisfying answer. Thus, they invented an explanation that relied upon superior knowledge rather than a righteousness sought through human faith and divine grace.

One version of Gnostic belief taught that the enlightened man was supremely spiritual and was thus freed from being bound to the flesh. This meant whatever happened in the physical body could not affect the spiritual person. This translated into a lifestyle of gratuitous indulgence, sexual sins, and other vices. Since the one (body) could not affect the other (spirit), then there was no moral consequence for one's bodily behavior. Furthermore, there was no need for Christian love, virtuous deeds, or any other demonstrations of faith since these practices had no effect on one's spiritual existence.[10]

John repeatedly denounces Gnosticism throughout his epistle. He presents himself as an eyewitness of Jesus *in the flesh* (refuting a Gnostic idea that He was merely an illusion). He also declares, with the authority of an apostle appointed *by* Jesus, that He (Jesus) is the Son of God, supported by the testimony of the Holy Spirit (2:20, 27, 5:6–8) and God Himself (5:9). Furthermore, he maintains no one can enter spiritual fellowship with God (the Father, Son, and Holy Spirit) unless he accepts the apostolic teaching concerning Jesus *as* the Christ *in the flesh*. Thus, John's epistle does bear direct refutations of Gnosticism:

- There is no compatibility between sin and righteousness, or the practicing sinner and the faithful Christian (1:5–10, 3:4–10, 5:18). Gnostics claim that a faithful Christian (as they describe one) *can* practice sin, since it is inconsequential to his relationship with God.
- Those who love God will keep His commandments (3:24, 5:1–2). Gnostics claim this is unnecessary, since deeds done in the body have no effect on the soul.
- One who denies that Jesus (the Man) is the Christ (the Son of God) is not in league with Christ, but is an "antichrist" (2:22, 4:1–3, 15).
- The water, blood, and Spirit testify that Jesus is the Son of God in the flesh (5:5–12). (See comments on that section for clarification.)
- Those who listen to the apostolic teaching, specifically from John himself, are of God; those who do not are of the world and in error (4:1–6).

But we should not look upon John's epistle *only* as a denouncement of Gnosticism. In the process of refuting error, John also defines, clarifies, and boldly proclaims divine truth. He provides the earnest believer with what are some of the clearest and most powerful declarations of the Christian life, love, and righteousness found in the NT.

Themes and Style of Writing: *First John* has numerous contrasting themes, often with very pointed conclusions. John provides Christians with an understanding of how to walk in fellowship with God—what needs to be done as well as avoided. Directly connected to this is the confidence that believers can have for trusting in God's help, especially through the avenue of prayer (5:13–15).

John consistently counters positive appeals with the negative ones—in essence, "If you walk with God, then you will be with Him; if you walk with the world, then you will be destroyed along with it." He offers no third alternative, and says it is impossible to walk with God *and* the world all at once. Fellowship with God, then, is the result of a real, functional, and covenant-bound relationship between Him and the one cleansed by the blood of Jesus (1:7). In sharp contrast is the one who "does not know God" (4:8), regardless of what he or she says (1:6, 8, 10, 2:4, etc.). Other contrasting themes include:

- Light versus darkness (1:5).
- Love versus hatred and murder (2:9–11, 4:8).
- Truth versus error (4:6).
- "Born of God" versus "in the world" (2:16, 5:4).
- "Children of God" versus "children of the devil" (3:10).
- Confidence in the Judgment versus fear of punishment (2:28, 4:17).
- Keeping God's commandments versus lawlessness (2:3, 3:4).
- Practicing righteousness versus practicing sin (3:7–8).
- Abiding in God (or, God abiding in the believer) versus abiding in death (3:14, 4:12).
- Spiritual life versus spiritual death (3:14).

John is very black-and-white: there is no "gray area" or moral confusion in his teaching. He says, in essence, "You are either *this*, or you are *that*." Factors that determine whether you are "this" or "that" begin with God but end with a person's own decisions. In other words, God lays down the commandments that define fellowship with Him, and these are binding, non-negotiable, and yet "not burdensome" (5:3).

One who claims to have this fellowship must live accordingly, which is also consistent with how Jesus Himself lived (2:6). It is impossible for a person to live a life of spiritual duplicity—to walk in light *and* darkness, to love God *and* hate his brother, to practice righteousness *and* practice sin, etc.—and be in good standing with God. Such a person is not merely confused, John says, but is "a liar" (used five times) and is identified with Satan rather than with God.

Another contrast underlying the entirety of *1 John* is between that of Jesus Christ (and His apostles) and Satan (and *his* apostles, the "antichrists"). Christ is the believer's model example of how to live, love, and practice righteousness. Satan is the complete antithesis of this, teaching people how to lie, hate, practice sin, and be deceived. Christ is a life-giver and Advocate; Satan is a murderer and accuser. Christ and His apostles are "from God" (4:5); those who practice sin are children of Satan (3:7–10). Christ appeases God's wrath through His self-sacrifice (2:1–2); Satan incites God's wrath by defying Him and deceiving the world (5:19).

There are several statements as well concerning the Holy Spirit (3:24, 4:2, 13, 5:6, and 5:8). The role of the Spirit is to consecrate, protect, and provide testimony for the believer. He also identifies those who are *true* apostles (the authoritative "we" in John's epistle) and those who are "false prophets" (4:1–3). John says nothing to indicate a *miraculous* working of the Spirit (i.e., in the form of spiritual gifts or actual miracles). Instead, the Spirit's role is provided for *all* who abide in God rather than the proportionately limited number of Christians to whom miraculous gifts had been imparted.

All said, John's theme is summed up in 5:13: "These things I have written to you who believe in the name of the Son of God, so that you may know that you have eternal life" (compare John 20:31). John wants his reading audience—faithful Christians—to *know* and *believe* life in God's name is not only *possible* but is made *real* and *doable* through the work of Jesus Christ.

The style of John's epistle is difficult to outline, map, or diagram. John often introduces a new subject or theme, then goes away from it for a while, only to return to that first subject with an entirely new or fresh emphasis. This pattern is more cyclic or spiraling than linear or goal oriented. Bible scholars have tried to explain this in the following way:

> This letter is built like an inverted pyramid or cone. The basic apex is laid down in 1:1–4; then the upward broadening begins. Starting with 1:5–10, the base rises and expands and continues in ever-widening circles as one new pertinent thought joins the preceding thought. One block is not laid beside the other so that joints are made. There are really no joints, not even where the new thoughts are introduced. The line of thought simply spirals in rising, widening circles until all is complete.[11]

This kind of literary structure makes *1 John* challenging to outline, but not difficult to read or understand. In fact, there is a great deal of intentional repetition of ideas in John's writing that reinforce important subjects in the mind of the reader, so that when he (the reader) is finished reading this epistle, he is left with a crystallized understanding of God's will for him (in contrast to Satan's scheming).

General Outline

- Introduction or Prologue (1:1–4)
- Walking in the Light of God (1:5–10)
- The "New Commandment" to Love (2:1–14)
- The Promise of Eternal Life (2:15–29)
- Children of God and Children of the Devil (3:1–10)
- "Love One Another" (3:11–24)
- The Spirit of Truth and the Spirit of Error (4:1–6)
- "God Is Love" (4:7–21)
- Jesus Is the Christ, the Son of God (5:1–12)
- Praying with Confidence (5:13–21)

Prologue (1 John 1:1–4)

True to the character of the entire epistle, John opens in a most unusual manner (1:1–3). While this obviously parallels the opening statements of his gospel (John 1:1–3), there is something far more personal in the statements he uses now. The "we" most certainly refers to the original disciples-turned-apostles, all of whom were eyewitnesses and personal friends with Jesus the Man. But instead of saying, "*He* who was in the beginning," he says, "What [or, That] was from the beginning."[12] This provides a much broader focus than merely Jesus the flesh-and-blood Person; it also involves His mission, teaching, atoning sacrifice, and divine nature.

An Eyewitness to the Word (1:1–3): As an apostle who sat at the feet of Jesus and participated in His teaching, John speaks with great authority and perspective. If it is true that all the other apostles have already died by the time John wrote this epistle, then he remains the only living link between the earthly life of Jesus and His intimate circle of disciples. He uses this profound position, then, to affirm that *the person Jesus* was most certainly *the Eternal Life*—not two different Personages, but the same. Thus (1:1):

- **"What [or, That] was from the beginning":** this necessarily implies the pre-existence of Jesus Christ. "The beginning" cannot be limited merely to Jesus' physical birth, since He was (first) "with the Father and [then] manifested to us" (1:2)—i.e., He once dwelt face-to-face with God, and then He "became flesh" (compare with John 1:1–3, 14–18). This means "the beginning" is the point in time when *mortal human beings* finally beheld Him in His earthly manifestation.
- **"what [or, that] we have heard":** John is a primary witness to whatever Jesus said or taught, far outranking the credentials of those who rival him (see 4:4–6).
- **"what [or, that] we have seen with our eyes":** not only did John *hear* Jesus speak, he also *saw* Him in the flesh, and saw His miracles performed in their very presence. Thus, he echoes what he and Peter boldly stated before the Jewish Council so many years before: "[W]

e cannot stop speaking about what we have seen and heard" (Acts 4:20).

- **"what [or, that] we have looked at and touched with our own hands"**: Some Gnostics believed that Jesus was a phantom (see "Introduction"), but John not only saw and heard Jesus; he also touched His physical body (compare Luke 24:39). Thus, John affirms authoritatively: Jesus was a living and historical person; He spoke, and He was heard; He dwelt among men and had physical contact with them; those who were His personal companions examined Him closely and testified for certain He was *real*.
- **"concerning the Word of life"**: When God *speaks* a "word," things come into existence that did not exist before (Heb. 11:3, 2 Peter 3:5, etc.). But God did not speak His Son into existence. Christ is not a created being; He comes *from the very midst* of God, as an exact representation of the Father Himself (John 14:7–10, Col. 2:9, Heb. 1:3, etc.). As "the Word," Christ is the physical, visible, and earthly manifestation of God "in the flesh" (1 Tim. 3:16), a revealed Personage of the Godhead. This "Word" is "of life": not just a message *about* life with God, but a Person who has full authority to *impart* this life ("I am the resurrection and the life"—John 11:25).

"[A]nd the life [Christ] was manifested ..." (1:2). This parenthetical verse further underscores what has been said: the Word who has always existed face-to-face with the Father (as John 1:1 literally implies) has become a physical, flesh-and-blood reality. He was heard, seen, and felt; He spoke, taught, and revealed; He "dwelt among us, and we saw His glory, glory as of the only begotten [Son] from the Father, full of grace and truth" (John 1:14). John is an eyewitness of this manifestation of God's Son, as were the other apostles (the "we" and "us" in this verse).

Since the apostles had fellowship with the Son, they had fellowship with the Father (1:3). Christ Himself promised this: "he who loves Me will be loved by My Father" (John 14:21). John says, in effect, "We apostles have enjoyed fellowship with the Father, and you can join us in that fellowship when you abide in our teaching concerning His Son."[13] John identifies what *kind* of fellowship he (and the others) enjoyed with Jesus—a real, tangible, and intimate fellowship. "What we proclaim to you" is this message: the one who abides (and remains) in the apostolic teaching concerning Christ, His gospel, the terms and conditions of fellowship, truth, etc., will enjoy communion with God.

Here (in 1:3) John specifically identifies who he is talking about: "His [the Father's] Son Jesus Christ." This harmonizes three identities: Son of God = Jesus the Man = Christ (Messiah) the Redeemer of prophecy. This also confirms Jesus' rightful relationship with God the Father, which is one of the overriding themes of this epistle:

- Redeeming blood of the Son (1:7, 2:2, 4:10).
- Fellowship of the believer with the Son (1:7).
- Mission of the Son (3:8).
- God's testimony of His Son (5:20).
- Eternal life being a gift of God's Son (5:11–12).
- The Second Coming of the Son (2:28).

The Fullness of Joy (1:4): "These things we write, so that our joy may be made complete" (1:4).[14] The "we" pronoun still refers to the apostles, even though most if not all of them are dead at the time of John's writing. Nonetheless, though these men are dead, and their office ended, their *teaching* continues to live on as an ever-present message of salvation and hope. At this point, John serves as the living spokesman for this body of men to whom Christ entrusted the revealing of this gospel message.

Lesson One
Walking in the Light of God
(1 John 1:5–10)

God Is Light (1:5): John anticipates the natural question, "If you heard the Word speak, what did He say?" Thus, John responds: "This is the message we have heard from Him …" (1:5). In the gospels, Jesus declared *Himself* to be the Light, not the Father (John 3:19, 8:12, etc.). But there is no contradiction here: just as God sent Jesus *as* the "Light of the world," brought a message *of* light (Mat. 4:12–16), and bore the "exact representation" of His Father *in* light (Heb. 1:3), so "God is Light"—the One from whom the "Light of the world" was sent.

Notice John does not say, "God *dwells* in light" (although this also is true—1 Tim. 6:16), nor does he say, "God is merely *filled* with light" (although this also is true), nor "*a* light" (which is *not* true, given His exclusive and unique nature), but that "God is Light." John is not speaking metaphorically here, but positively and absolutely: this is a defining statement of the absolute and divine nature of God. "Light" is necessary for life, and especially spiritual life. It represents divine glory, transcendent truth, and moral purity (or holiness).

But what is this "Light"? It cannot be physical light, since God is not even of the physical realm, but is above it, outside of it, and superior to it. We cannot define God by physical means, but the NT writers (and Jesus Himself) used physical qualities or properties to give us a relative understanding of who God is. We should never press the comparison too far, nor limit God to what we know of physical light. John does not say that God is a physical light; he says that *all* light—physical, moral, and spiritual—emanates from God's essential nature.

Walking in God's Light (1:6–10): "God is Light" and He is "the Father of lights" in whom there is "no shifting shadow" (James ` 1:17)—there is no change *in* Him, and nothing can *cause* Him to change. Since God has literally no speck or trace of darkness in Himself, one cannot "walk in the darkness" while claiming fellowship with Him (1:6; compare John 8:12). To "walk" indicates a regular practice of something or a habitual lifestyle and is a common metaphor in the epistles. A person cannot claim to have communion with the Father who lives in such a way that violates His essential nature.

No doubt John is thinking of actual individuals he has encountered who have tried to do just this. Yet it is impossible to join God's holy Light with "the darkness." The one who claims to do so—and John's editorial "we" indicates that it is possible for *anyone* (Christian or otherwise) to make such a claim—lies against himself, the teachings of the apostles, the teaching of Jesus Christ, the revelation of the Holy Spirit, and the divine nature of God Himself.

"[B]ut if we walk in the Light …" (1:7a). Having first revealed the negative condition of one who *lies* against the truth, John now shows the positive condition of one who lives in *agreement* with it. "[A]s He Himself is in the Light" serves to qualify or modify John's statement: not, "If we *think* we are walking in the light," or, "If we are walking in what *we consider* to be 'the light,'" but (to paraphrase), "If we are walking in a manner fully consistent with God, who *is* Light." It is common (and increasingly popular today) for someone to speak of his "fellowship" with God, having founded this upon his personal take on the gospel but not the actual teaching of it. Yet, when we have fellowship with God, then we also have fellowship with all others who also have fellowship with God.

"Fellowship" necessarily implies a partnership, mutual participation, sharing (in something), alliance, or communion.[15] This is expressed negatively in 2 Cor. 6:14–16a: we cannot be "bound together with" or form (a) "partnership," "fellowship," or "harmony," or have anything "in common" or make any "agreement" with God (Light) and whatever opposes Him (unbelievers, lawlessness, darkness, Satan, unbelievers, or idolatry). Positively, we *can* and *do* have fellowship with all parties who are walking in the light, including "the Light" (God) Himself.

"[A]nd the blood of Jesus His Son cleanses us from all sin" (1:7b).[16] Christ's blood provides the *necessary* and *absolute* cleansing of the soul from all darkness and defilement of sin (Eph. 1:7, Col. 1:13–14). This statement necessarily implies specific demands upon our fellowship with believers *and* our walking in the Light. In other words, such fellowship and walking are not subjectively or arbitrarily determined but are the result of cleansing with Christ's blood. This requires that one has obeyed God's commandments concerning this forgiveness of his sins and has become a Christian according to His gospel.

It is impossible to receive forgiveness of sins through the blood of Christ without becoming a Christian. Just as the shedding of Jesus' blood is real and historical, so is the sinful act committed by the one who now needs this blood's cleansing. Jesus' blood "cleanses us from *all* sin"—not just some sins, but all: we are either defiled with sin or we are cleansed from sin; we cannot be both at the same time.[17]

But this cleansing also necessitates that one takes personal responsibility for his sin. Thus, "If we say that we have no sin, we are deceiving ourselves and the truth is not in us" (1:8). This does not mean, "If we say that we have *never* sinned," but (the context demands), "If we say that we are presently *not* in sin (even though we are walking in darkness)." Since walking in the darkness is inconsistent with walking in the Light, the only way in which one can justify any reconciliation of the two "walks" is through self-deception: a person must lie to himself, violate his conscience, and profess a false faith.

However, when we *confess* our sins—i.e., when we take responsibility for the darkness in which we have participated—then "He is faithful and righteous to forgive us our sins and to cleanse us from all unrighteousness" (1:9). To "confess" means "to say the same thing or word as" someone else[18]; in this case, it means to speak in agreement with God. The thing agreed upon here is the true nature of the confessor's situation: he *did* sin; he *did* partake of the darkness; he *is* guilty; he *has* violated God's commandments; etc. In other words, we are to own up to what we have done and plead with God for His mercy, grace, and forgiveness. We make this confession through prayer to God, and (if necessary) in a verbal admittance to others.

"God is faithful" is an expression used other times in the NT (1 Cor. 1:9, 10:13, 2 Cor. 1:18, etc.). "Faithful" in this context means trustworthy, dependable, reliable, and sure. God will not disappoint the one who puts his faith in Him—in this case, to cleanse him of his sins—because "He remains faithful" (2 Tim. 2:13) to what He has promised us. "John states this truth for the sake of the fullest assurance of his readers against all false argumentation of the liars who scorn the blood of God's Son."[19]

John now returns to the negative scenario proposed in 1:8 ("If we say that we have not sinned …"), yet with a slightly different emphasis (1:10). In 1:8, John refers to a present sin that one denies having committed; in 1:10, he refers to one's claim to have *never sinned at all*. Such a claim puts one on par with God Himself, in whom there is no sin and never *has* sinned. Not only this, but "we make Him a liar" because He says we *have* sinned (Rom. 3:23).

This does not mean we *literally* make God a liar. Our accusations or insinuations against God cannot alter His eternal nature; we cannot successfully make God a liar any more than we can successfully mock Him (Gal. 6:7). John means we *accuse* God of being a liar (because we refuse to accept His evaluation of our sinful condition) when in fact it is *we* who are lying against the truth of His word (James 3:14, 1 John 5:10). Those who lie against the truth/word proves that "His word is not in" them.

Questions

1.) According to John (1:5), what is the *first principle* regarding fellowship with God?

    a. Why is this so important to understand? (What if we miss it?)

    b. What bearing does this have on how Christians think and live?

2.) What is "the darkness" to which John refers in 1:6? Is this just the absence of God, or is it something more specific than this? (Consider Luke 11:34–35, 22:53, John 1:5, and 3:19 in your answer.)

3.) What does it mean to "walk in the Light" (1:7)? Can a person walk in light and darkness all at once? Is it enough for a person to *believe* he is walking in "the Light," or is something more required of him to substantiate this?

Lesson Two
The "New Commandment" to Love (1 John 2:1–14)

Christ's Advocacy for Believers (2:1–2): John has provided both sides of the coin, so to speak: he has shown the false position of one who walks in the darkness but claims to be "in the Light"; and he has shown the true position of one who *was* in the darkness but confesses his sin, pleads for forgiveness, and is cleansed by the blood of Christ. This explanation is the reason for his having written this letter in the first place (2:1).

"My little children" is John's tender appeal to his fellow Christians; he speaks with a fatherly perspective, providing guidance, instruction, and admonition to his "children." This is likely because of his elderly age, his authority as an apostle, and the fact that some (or many?) of those to whom he is writing know him and may have been taught the gospel by him.

First, John states the preventive nature of his letter: "I am writing these things to you so that you may not sin" (2:1). This is his primary objective—not to deal with sin after the fact, but to proactively steer the believer from even engaging in such behavior. However, this will not always be successful. Thus, he provides a recourse for the Christian who has unwisely chosen otherwise: "And if anyone sins …" The "anyone" here (coupled with the editorial "we") refers to those who are already within the body of Christ. He is not giving anyone *license* to sin (Rom. 6:1–2) or to have a relaxed *attitude* toward sin. John is being realistic, not passive; he is not excusing sin, but he does explain the recourse a Christian has when he has committed it.

It is natural for Christians to want to avoid confessing sin before the Father. Feelings of guilt, shame, unworthiness, and disappointment in our own behavior make such confession difficult and uncomfortable. Yet, John assures believers that we have One who will be there to help us—"Jesus Christ the righteous." Even though we have sinned, He provides atonement for our sins in His blood. His sacrificial death provides the ransom necessary to remove our condemnation; His blood provides the atonement necessary to fulfill God's demand for justice against us.

In this role, Jesus serves as an "Advocate." In classical Greek, an advocate was literally "one who pleads another's cause before a judge; a pleader; counsel for the defense; legal assistant; intercessor."[20] Jesus provides advocacy for the believer who has sinned against God and is doing what He requires of him to rectify this problem. The implication, however, is that he *cannot* rectify the problem on his own. Jesus' role as his Advocate is not just to facilitate the process; rather, it is to make it even possible.

"[A]nd He Himself is the propitiation for our sins …" (2:2). "Propitiation" refers to an appeasement, satisfaction, or expiation. In the present case, the thing appeased is God's wrath as the result of our sin since His wrath is "against all ungodliness and unrighteousness" (Rom. 1:18). It is not Christians who offer blood sacrifices to God to appease Him of their sins, but it is God's own Son who has offered His blood for this purpose. Thus, instead of us producing the means of our own propitiation, Jesus Christ takes care of this Himself. In fact, reconciliation with God cannot happen by any other means. It is only through His blood, and no other agent, which will appease or satisfy God's wrath (Rom. 5:9).

"[A]nd not for ours only, but … the whole world" (2:2b). God will only apply Christ's blood to those who call upon the Lord for salvation. He never saves people "anyway" who will not turn to Him in faith; He never forgives people "anyway" who refuse to fulfill the conditions necessary for that forgiveness (i.e., faith, obedience, humility, confession, and repentance). Yet, it remains true that His blood is *sufficient* for the cleansing of all men's souls; His blood is not only for a certain number of preordained recipients, nor is His blood unable to perform in the cleansing of some sins over others. Thus, if the entire world came to Christ for forgiveness, His blood can forgive every single person, regardless of the number of sins or the awfulness of the crimes committed.

Consistency between Profession and Lifestyle (2:3–6): Fellowship with God requires the believer to walk in the light of His holiness, truth, and righteousness. We cannot know God—and "know" here means to *experience* Him in a personal and practical manner—unless we keep His commandments (2:3). This is a conditional "if ... then" statement: if we will not be keepers of His commandments, then we cannot be sharers in His fellowship. It is necessary to put into practice what we have seen in Him and learned from Him; otherwise, a person "is a liar, and the truth is not in Him" (2:4).

"But whoever keeps His word ..." (2:5)—now John reveals the positive state of being of the person who obeys God's commandments. "[I]n him the love of God has truly been perfected"—i.e., the love we have *learned* from God is reaching its objective. John speaks in the idealistic and finished sense: one who is a commandment-keeper must also be one who has learned and put into practice the proper motivation for doing this. "By this we know that we are in Him"—i.e., He abides in us, and we abide in Him.

To abide [lit., dwell, remain] in Christ—our heavenly example—we must live ("walk") as He lived (2:6). This does not mean we need to be flawless, filled with heavenly wisdom, and miracle-working; such things are impossible for any of us. Rather, it means we need to adopt His heart, imitate His love, support His cause, and pattern our behavior after His own (Eph. 5:1–2). The person who does this will most certainly abide in God's love; the one who refuses to do this does not have the love of God, no matter what he says or how passionately he defends otherwise. Having deceived himself, he then attempts to deceive others.

The Commandment to Love (2:7–11): Now John becomes more specific about what this "love of God" really is (2:7–11): demonstrations of godly love toward one's "brother." Before stating this directly, however, John explains the foundation for it. The "old" commandment—i.e., the keeping of God's law—has been known to Christians (and the believing Israelites in particular) "from the beginning." In other words, this is a first principle and fundamental teaching. "[T]he word which you have heard" (2:7) is the gospel message which was preached to them (Heb.

2:1–4). The "new commandment," however, is summed up in Christ and His love (2:8a; see John 13:34–35). It is "new" because:

- it has been raised to a completely new standard in the life of Jesus.
- of the extent to which it reached (in Jesus' love for *sinners*).
- of the lengths to which it has gone (in Jesus' *sacrifice* for the entire world).
- of how it challenged men to live (upon hearing of Jesus' love in the gospel.)[21]

Love is the basis for all of God's commandments; at the same time, it is also the epitome of one's commandment-keeping life. Love, then, is both the base and the capstone of all of Gods' laws (Mat. 22:37–40, Rom. 13:10, and Gal. 5:14). This love "is true in Him [Christ]" (2:8b)—because it comes from God and has been exemplified in Christ. However, it is also "true … in you" who believe in and follow Him. In such people, "the darkness" of sin, self-deception, and worldliness are "passing away," and the "true Light is already shining" in them.

In contrast—because John loves to provide contrasts, and everything about God is indeed a glaring contrast with everything else—the person who claims to be filled with God's "Light" but "hates his brother" remains in "the darkness" (2:9). "Hate," in the context in which John uses it throughout this epistle, does not only require an active hostility or loathing toward another person. Instead—and regardless of any visible negative demonstration—it refers to the withholding of one's love from another. Specifically, it is the withholding of *godly love* toward one who himself has fellowship with God (a "brother" in the faith; a member of the "household of God"—1 Tim. 3:15). "Until now"—meaning, unless things change—this "so-called brother" (1 Cor. 5:11) is swallowed by the satanic darkness of lies and hypocrisy rather than walking in the pure and brilliant light of God.[22]

In 2:10–11, John summarizes the problem clearly. Living in the Light provides godly love, a prescription for godly living, and spiritual illumination. He "loves his brother" not with mere words, but with deeds and in truth (see 3:18). He is not only himself filled with God's light, but he also reflects this light for the benefit of others. The one who is enlightened by God also draws near to Him; the one who hates is blinded *by* his hate and darkness and cannot even "see" God. As love is associated with light, so hate is associated with darkness. The one who *claims* to be filled with God's light but refuses to show love to his brother is himself stumbling (sinning) in the darkness and causes others to stumble as well (with his poor example and godless behavior).[23]

Encouragement for Christians (2:12–14): John now makes general appeals to separate groups of people (2:12–14). This section serves as a conclusion to what he has just said as well as preamble to what he is about to say. He writes with an elderly and fatherly concern; it is clearly the words of an older man who is wise to Satan's deceit. It is admonishing in nature, carrying both encouragement and warnings all at once. Yet, John seems to be categorizing his remarks relative to the spiritual maturity of his readers, not to any specific gender or age group.[24] John makes two sets of comments to each group: the first set is introduced with "I am writing …"; the second, with "I have written …" The present verb tense ("I am writing") indicates John's original purpose in addressing them; the past verb tense ("I have written") puts the responsibility upon the groups themselves, as in, "This is how I expect you to respond to what I have said."

First, John addresses the entire group: "little children" (2:12, 2:13c). Obviously, this tender expression refers to his "children" in the faith, men and women added to the body of Christ, in part because of John's own teaching, apostleship, and personal example. In contrast to the following expressions, however, "children" here may refer to those more recently added than the others; they are younger in the faith, and thus "children" by comparison.

Despite their inexperience, they have been forgiven "for His name's sake." They "know the Father" (2:13c), but they must not become presumptuous in, or careless with, this knowledge. Knowing God must never reduce the need for or take the place of obedience to the Father's commandments.

Second, John addresses the "fathers" among the group—not literal fathers, and not even literally (or necessarily) men, but those who are spiritually mature and have a long record of proven obedience to Jesus Christ (2:13a, 2:14a). (The Greek word for "fathers" includes older men *and* women [i.e., parents], as expressed in the masculine sense.[25])

Because of their maturity in Christ, and their longevity in the brotherhood, they "know Him who has been from the beginning"—a likely reference to those of the same generation as Jesus Himself. In his repeat of his statement to this group, John says, in effect, "*Since you know Christ, you will understand why I am writing and what I am saying.*" Because they have experience and maturity, they also are aware of the dangers facing the brotherhood (and younger Christians in particular), and so they ought to provide a fatherly oversight to those of lesser experience. Thus, these "fathers" are expected to reinforce John's teaching to these other Christians.

Third, John addresses believers whom he refers to as "young men"—again, not exclusively young males, but young believers (2:13b, 2:14b). John's use of masculine words follows the expected male-dominant language of his day. We detect a slightly different emphasis with these people than with the older Christians. While the older may have a deeper fellowship with God, the younger nonetheless have had victories and successes in "overcoming the evil one [Satan]." This is neither to say that they do not have fellowship (for indeed they do) nor that older believers have not had their own victories (for indeed they have).

However, there is an implied difference in the level of growth and maturity. John does not credit the "young men" *personally* for these victories but gives credit instead to "the word of God [which] abides in you"—this is the source of their strength. In effect, John says, "*You are strong, and God's word does abide in you, and this is why you are able to overcome—but do not forget the true source of your strength (and begin to rely upon your own strength instead).*"

Questions

1.) Does Jesus only advocate for us when we are in trouble (2:1–2), or does He advocate for us even when we think things are going well? Please explain.

2.) Is commandment-keeping all there is to "knowing" God (2:3–5)? If so, then are we saved because we keep commandments? If not, then why does John lay so much stress on the *need* to keep commandments?

3.) Does a Christian only "hate" his "brother" when he holds him in deep contempt and wishes for his demise (2:9, 11)?

    a. Likewise, must a Christian be best friends with and give full attention to every "brother" to "love" him?

    b. What does John really mean by "hate" or "love" in the context of this epistle—and how do you know this?

Lesson Three
The Promise of Eternal Life
(1 John 2:15–29)

Love for the World versus Love for the Father (2:15–17): There are numerous profound statements in John's first epistle, but one of the most notable of these is in the next few verses (2:15–17). "Do not love the world …" (2:15)—the "world" here refers to the self-serving, satanic, and boastful human spirit that exalts itself against God. To "love the world" means to put one's confidence in this life; have one's affections in the world's material things; and give more attention to (really, *worship* of) this life and/or its material things than to God. To "love the world" makes people insensitive to God's kindness, mercy, and grace; they are unconcerned with what God has done (and what He promises to do) to save them from spiritual ruin. "The 'world' which God loves is mankind; that which man is forbidden to love is an evil order or sphere."[26]

Thus, "If anyone loves the world, the love of the Father is not in him"—i.e., such a person has filled his heart with darkness, self-deception, and false hope rather than with God's love for him. Just as it is impossible to serve two masters (Mat. 6:24), so it is impossible to devote one's heart to the world and to God at the same time.

Then John clearly differentiates between one's "love" for the world and love which comes from God (2:16). These are two incompatible loves; they cannot peacefully coexist; they have nothing in common (2 Cor. 6:14–16, Gal. 5:16–17). "The world"—just as "the darkness"—is under the wicked influence of Satan; just as Satan is antagonistic to Christ, so the world is antagonistic to His church. "The world" implies ignorance, illegitimacy, and perversion (of justice, morality, and relationships).

John had praised the "little children," "young men," and "fathers" for their faith in God, but this does not mean all the danger has passed. The world continues to exert a powerful influence upon the human spirit; one's love for God is constantly tested and even assaulted by one's carnal and satanic desires:

- "lust of the flesh"—in essence, all sensuous (including sexual) or carnal desires that seek gratification through sinful activity. "Lust" refers to any strong desire, longing, or craving, whether wicked or not.[27] Often, however, this powerful desire ("lust") has a negative connotation, as it does in the present text (2:16). In this case, John links this with covetousness, greed, fornication, sexual adultery, and debauchery.
- "lust of the eyes"—specifically, the strong desire for the things we can *see*, which are limited to this world and are temporal in nature (2 Cor. 4:18). We are often tempted to sin through our worldly vision (literally and figuratively) (compare Mat. 5:28). The eyes are, in a sense, a window into a person's soul; when they are corrupted (with lust to do evil), then what comes into that soul is darkness (Luke 11:34–36).
- "boastful pride [lit., boastfulness] of life"—i.e., the human desire for conquest, control, domination, independence (from restraint), and all arrogance or boasting in oneself. Boasting assumes one's control or mastery of something, as determined by one's own human power, strength, or ability. Thus, it is a cocky, self-confident attitude based upon age, material wealth, status, personal ability, or personal knowledge.

John then reveals the futility of giving one's love, devotion, or attention to the world rather than to the Father. "The world is passing away, and also its lusts" (2:17a): all the loves and boasts that belong to the ungodly world will pass away *with* the world. The idea of the world "passing away" has a double meaning.

- **First**, it refers to the hopeless future of the unrighteous: just as earthly life passes away in death, so one's spiritual life passes away in his pursuit of a spiritually dead world. Nothing good will ever become of the person who worships "the world" rather than God.
- **Second**, it refers to the end of the physical world itself (2 Peter 3:10–12). Whatever is "seen" is temporal; only the invisible world—invisible to us, anyway—is eternal in nature (2 Cor. 4:18). As the source for carnal desire disappears, so will those desires themselves—and so will those who filled their hearts with such desires.

"[B]ut the one who does the will of God lives forever" (2:17b): not only will such a person survive the destruction of the unrighteous *and* the physical system, but he will also dwell with God in *His* world forever. Just as God's righteousness will have no end, so will those who seek that righteousness (Mat. 6:33); just as God's world (heaven) will never "pass away," so will those who put their treasure in it (Mat. 6:19–21). In God's world are all the things this present world cannot offer: light, life, blessing, honor, holiness, salvation, immortality, priceless treasures, peace, and endless joy.

Warnings about Antichrists (2:18–24): In this next section (2:18–24), John continues to contrast those who "abide" or "remain" with God (and the teachings of God) and those who are "antichrists" because they "went out [or, away] from us." Simply put, John contrasts those in fellowship with God and those whose fellowship is with the world. "The last hour" (2:18a) is synonymous with the "last days" as used by other NT writers (Acts 2:17, Heb. 1:2, 1 Peter 1:20, and James 5:3). Generally speaking, "last days" refers to the Christian era, the dispensation of human history in which the gospel of Christ is preached to the world. Being the *last* days indicates there will be no more earthly dispensations to follow; "then comes the end" (1 Cor. 15:24).

But "last days" or "last hour" also carries a foreboding and impending sense, as John implies: it is the time (or age) in which false prophets and false teaching will also arise concurrent with the proclamation of the gospel (as Paul also uses the expression in 2 Tim. 3:1). "From this"—the appearance of these false brethren—"we know that it *is* the last hour" (2:18b, emphasis added).

"Antichrist" (2:18)—possibly a word John coined himself—is transliterated from the Greek [*antichristos*] and means an opponent of Christ.[28] It is a term hugely misunderstood or misrepresented in modern end-of-the-world parlance. John is the only one who uses the "antichrist" term, and only in his epistles. Putting together the four times he uses this word reveals who and what he describes:

- "Children, it is the last hour; and just as you heard that antichrist is coming, even now many antichrists have appeared; from this we

know that it is the last hour" (1 John 2:18).
- "Who is the liar but the one who denies that Jesus is the Christ? This is the antichrist, the one who denies the Father and the Son" (1 John 2:22).
- "By this you know the Spirit of God: every spirit that confesses that Jesus Christ has come in the flesh is from God; and every spirit that does not confess Jesus is not from God; this is the spirit of the antichrist, of which you have heard that it is coming, and now it is already in the world" (1 John 4:2–3).
- "For many deceivers have gone out into the world, those who do not acknowledge Jesus Christ as coming in the flesh. This is the deceiver and the antichrist" (2 John 7).

The "spirit of the antichrist" is the spirit of false teachers who pose as genuine believers but reject the teaching of the Father, Son, and Holy Spirit. Such a person makes himself an *opponent* of Christ—he is *anti*-Christ—rather than a follower of Him (Mat. 12:30). Specifically, however, John is addressing those who are teachers (or promoters) of this false gospel rather than the many who will simply accept this propaganda in ignorance.

Such teachers "went out from us, but they were not really of us" (2:19)—i.e., these men had started out professing to be Christians, having submitted to the authority of the apostles (the "us" to which John refers). John implies there may have been something defective in the hearts of these people, and they may never have been sincere in their devotion to Christ at all. Regardless, they did not remain subject to the apostolic teaching but embraced a false gospel instead, then began peddling this false message as though it were genuine. It is this situation that provides the basis for John's writing of this epistle. He has a sacred responsibility as an apostle of Christ not only to teach what is true but also to expose those who are false (compare Titus 1:9). "[T]hey went out" is another way of saying "they ceased to be genuine," and thus true followers of Christ have no business listening to them (compare 1 Cor. 14:37–38).

"But you have an anointing from the Holy One" (2:20)—i.e., those who remain with (or abide in) the true teaching about Jesus Christ have the indwelling of the Holy Spirit.[29] "Anointing" here is used figuratively to describe how Christians are set apart, consecrated, and sanctified by the Spirit (1 Cor. 6:11, 2 Cor. 1:21–22, Eph. 1:13–14, 1 Peter 1:2, etc.). It is the Holy Spirit who provides *proof* of Jesus' divine nature (through the demonstrations of miracles); testifies of Jesus to the world (through the gospel message—John 16:8–11); and guides believers in the truth (Gal. 5:16). One who is filled with the Spirit cannot also be filled with the darkness of false teaching about Christ, since it is through the Spirit (i.e., His revealed word) that we know the true nature of Jesus Christ. The Spirit will never lead one into error who listens to His gospel and follows His divine leadership.

"[A]nd you all know" (2:20) can be taken two ways: "you all know" the Holy Spirit, since He indwells you; and/or "you all know" false teaching from God's truth, since the Spirit provides the transcendent standard by which all teaching is measured (see 4:1).[30] There is nothing here in the context of John's words that suggests he is talking about miraculous] gifts, but refers instead to the indwelling of the Spirit enjoyed by all who obey Christ and His gospel (Acts 5:32, Rom. 8:9, 1 Cor. 6:19–20, etc.).[31]

John further clarifies his reason for writing: it is not to accuse his readers of not knowing the truth, but to remind them that there is no compatibility between God's truth and these antichrists (2:21). Just as there is no darkness in light (recall 1:5), so there can be no lie in divinely revealed truth. The "lie" here specifically is the claim that Jesus, the flesh-and-blood Man, is not the Christ (Messiah), the only begotten Son of God (2:22). Again, this false position denies the testimonies of Jesus and the Father that affirm otherwise.

The one who denies the truth of Jesus' identity as the Christ is a "liar"—he is not simply confused or ignorant, but deliberately practices lying.[32] John states flatly that no one can "know" the Father except through His Son (2:23), and Jesus proved Himself to be God's Son (John 20:30–31). John admonishes his readers to "let that abide in you which you heard from the beginning" (2:24)—namely, the original and genuine word of truth (the gospel) which the apostles preached. Wherever the word of God abides, so will the Father and the Son abide.

The Confidence of Eternal Life (2:25–29): The word of God bears the promise Jesus made to all who believe and obey Him: eternal life (2:25). ("He" in this context refers to Jesus; see John 3:15–16.) It seems that John inserts this point here to remind his reading audience exactly what is at stake in choosing what to believe about Jesus. In swallowing the lies of antichrists, a person forfeits his eternal life with God; in remaining faithful to the apostolic teaching of Jesus, a person will receive eternal life from God. Those who are "trying to deceive you" (2:26) reveals a deception that implies not only a false teaching but also a false motive: a deliberate and malicious misrepresentation of God's word.

John returns to the "anointing" Christians have received from God (recall 2:20)—i.e., the indwelling of the Holy Spirit (2:27). One can only have this indwelling if he believes in the word of truth (the gospel) and is faithful to keep its commandments (recall 2:3). The Spirit of God will not lead the one in whom He indwells into error, deception, or lies of any kind. "[Y]ou have no need for anyone to teach you" does not mean "You know everything because you are Christians," for this would defeat the entire purpose for him to write them any instruction.

Instead, John means that believers do not need another *source* of teaching apart from (or instead of) what the Holy Spirit has revealed to Christ's apostles (Heb. 8:11). "His anointing"—i.e., the Spirit's indwelling resulting from one's acceptance of His teaching—will provide everything necessary for "life and godliness" (2 Peter 1:3). This teaching "is true and is not a lie" because it comes from God (the Light); there can be no darkness or falsehood in it. Whatever is of human origin, however, will bear the lies, inconsistencies, and contradictions common to men.

While the "anointing" refers to the Holy Spirit and "the truth" refers to the revealed word of God, John's emphasis remains on the One who has provided this anointing and revealed word: Jesus Christ. The ultimate proof that Jesus *is* the Christ will be when He (Jesus) appears again— His Second Coming. John's statement about His appearance is one of certainty, not speculation; John does not say, "if He appears" or "if He *were* to appear," but "*when* He appears" (2:28, emphasis added). Those who remain true to His word and thus "abide in Him" will have no need for shame or regret when He comes; herein is our "confidence."[33] John does not say *when* Jesus will return, only that His return is certain to happen and (thus) we should always be ready for it (compare 1 Thess. 5:1–6).

With this reference to the coming of Jesus Christ and the admonition to be prepared for that event, John now turns to the righteous character of Jesus Himself. As He is righteous, so we must also practice righteousness (2:29). "[I]f you know that He is righteous" is another way of saying "*Since* you know this (by the teaching that has come to you through His own apostles)." To be "born of Him" means to believe in Jesus Christ and to enter a covenant relationship with God through water (baptism) and sanctification of the Spirit (John 3:5). Only those who are born *of* God are made righteous *by* God; these also become *children* of God.

Questions

1.) Please explain what it means to "love the world" as John uses this phrase (2:15). Are Christians immune to this misdirected "love" simply because they *are* Christians?

2.) Many people believe the "antichrist" (often capitalized) is a specific historical person who, in our future, will incite a final global war between good and evil, ushering in the end of the world.

   a. What is John's definition of "antichrist" (2:18–23)?

   b. Do you think "antichrists" exist in the world today? In so-called "Christian" churches?

3.) John has much to say, both directly and indirectly, about having "confidence" in our relationship with God (2:28). Why is confidence critical to our endurance of faith and success in overcoming the world's darkness? (Consider Heb. 3:6, 4:16, 6:11, and 10:22 in your answer.)

Lesson Four
Children of God and Children of the Devil
(1 John 3:1–10)

Those Who Are Children of God (3:1–3): Identification as "children of God" is a privilege bestowed upon those who are born of Him (3:1). "Children" (or sons) in this usage implies the source of this status, without reference to physical age: our Father who is in heaven.[34]

The original Greek language here (in 3:1) is emphatic, as an exclamation: "See ... we are called children of God! And we are!" John speaks of this special relationship we have with God—not as mere slaves but as His friends (John 15:14), even His children (John 1:12–13)—as something unnatural and unexpected. This, not because it is surprising to see God's love poured out, but because we (who were once His enemies) are so undeserving of it.

> There is something here which we may well note. It is by the gift of God that a man becomes a child of God. By nature a man is the *creature* of God, but it is by grace that he *becomes* the child of God. There are two English words which are closely connected but whose meanings are widely different, *paternity* and *fatherhood*. *Paternity* describes a relationship in which a man is responsible for the physical existence of a child; *fatherhood* describes an intimate, loving, relationship. In the sense of *paternity* all men are children of God; but in the sense of *fatherhood* men are children of God only when he makes his gracious approach to them and they respond.[35]

God's love—really, this *kind* of love and the gracious *application* of it—is foreign to those who choose to live in moral darkness. Christ is the One who makes the fulfillment of this love—our salvation—possible (Rom. 5:8). Since the world "did not know Him [Christ]," therefore it will not (does not) understand our spiritual union with the Lord (John 15:18–

19, 1 Cor. 6:17). "The world is proud of its knowledge, but the real things worth knowing it does not know."[36]

But even though we are now (presently) children *of* God, and known *by* God, we do not yet look *like* God (3:2). That is, the world sees us in our human state—unglorified, imperfect, scarred by our experiences, and struggling in our faith. But it will not always be this way. In time, God will not only reveal that we *are* His children; He will also glorify us with the glory He now possesses.

While "it has not yet appeared" what this glory will look like, we know it is certain to come (1 Cor. 15:35–53). When Christ appears (in His Second Coming), we will see Him in *His* glory—not in His human form, but in His heavenly majesty, as befits a Divine Personage. And "we will be like Him"—i.e., we will be sharers in that glory, since we are now sharers in His fellowship (compare Phil. 3:20–21).[37]

"And everyone ... purifies himself, just as He is pure" (3:3)—in other words, God's promise is conditional: one must fix his hope on Christ *and* purify himself.[38] Even so, God extends this promise to *everyone* who does these, with no exceptions. One who refuses to purify himself cannot anticipate glorification with Christ but can only await an awful judgment (compare Heb. 10:26–31). Purification requires atonement from sins *and* consecration (of lifestyle) to God (2 Cor. 7:1, 1 Peter 1:15–16). Both parties—children of God and God Himself—are necessarily involved in the purification process (recall 1:7, 9). If this is done, then our hope of one day being "like Him [Christ]" will be realized—this is God's unfailing promise.

Practicing Sin versus Practicing Righteousness (3:4–10): Moral purity is not compatible with sinful behavior. One's outward actions will be consistent with his internal or spiritual nature, whether for good or evil (compare Mat. 12:33). In the next verses, John tells his readers:

- what sin is—the deliberate transgression of God's law (*any* law; see James 2:10); *lawlessness*.
- why sin is—the rejection of God's control of our lives in exchange for personal gratification.

- where sin comes from—Satan is the primary temptation for all sin in the world since he taught us to sin like he did "from the beginning."
- how sin is overcome—through Christ, who is powerful enough "to destroy the works of the devil."

"Everyone who practices sin" (3:4) refers to those who claim to "know God" (recall 2:3-4) but are walking in darkness, not in the light. Both scenarios—purifying oneself or practicing sin—are personal choices. "[S]in is lawlessness": those who practice sin have no regard or respect for God's law, just as one who is careless has no regard for care. "Lawlessness" [lit., without law] is defiance not only against law itself, but also the Lawgiver.[39] Thus, it is impossible to be in fellowship with God and defy Him at the same time; it is impossible to honor His law and deliberately break it at the same time.

Jesus "appeared" (i.e., came into our world—see Titus 2:11-14) to save us *from* sin, not so that we could continue to indulge in it (3:5; compare Rom. 6:1-2). "[I]n Him there is no sin"—an affirmative declaration to the sinless and innocent nature of Jesus (as in 2 Cor. 5:21, Heb. 4:15, 1 Peter 2:22, etc.). Since Jesus did not practice sin, those who conform to His holy nature must not either.

"No one who abides in Him sins ..." (3:6a)—in the present passage, John is *not* saying, "Christians must never sin," nor, "It is impossible for Christians *to* sin," since both propositions contradict the rest of the NT. Rather, he speaks (again) of the *practice* of sin—the habitual, recurring, and chronic indulgence of sinful activity for which there is no remorse and no repentance. Such a person has not "seen" Christ (as his Lord, since he does not follow Him; compare Luke 6:46) and has not "known" Him (i.e., has no experiential knowledge of fellowship with Him, as is evident by his unreformed behavior) (3:6b).

Those who practice righteousness identify with Christ; those who practice sin identify with "the devil" (3:7-10). John warns his reading audience not to be "deceived" into thinking otherwise. Specifically, John warns us not to let *others* deceive us. Likely, this warning refers to those Gnostics who believed that, since what happens in the flesh is of no consequence to the spirit, it is harmless to indulge in sinful behavior. John strongly counters this: those who practice sin are in league with Satan, not Christ (or the Father).[40] "[T]he devil has sinned from the beginning" (3:8)—likely, John refers to the beginning of humankind (compare John 8:44).[41]

In 3:5, John said that Jesus "appeared in order to take away sins"; here he says He appeared for the purpose of destroying "the works of the devil" (3:8). While Christ is the Creator of the physical world and humankind (all that is "very good"—Gen. 1:31), Satan is the creator (so to speak) of all that stands opposed to God—lies, murder, and sinful activity of every kind. Jesus came to destroy what we allow Satan to create *in us*; in the end, He will destroy Satan himself. "Destroy" here means, in context, to take away the power of (the devil's works).

"No one who is born of God practices sin ..." (3:9). This is simply a reverse statement of what John said earlier (recall 2:29). Both statements are true; both necessitate the same definition of sin *and* righteousness. Sin is what Satan does himself and incites others to do; righteousness is what Jesus does Himself and inspires others to do (if they wish to follow Him; recall 2:6). "His seed" (3:9) refers to the word of God (the gospel truth)—not as a mere assemblage of words, verses, and commandments, but as a *living* and *life-imparting* message. It is impossible for God's word (or truth, or Spirit) to indwell anyone who has not first been "born of God."

The new spiritual birth provides for the indwelling of God's "seed"—a seed producing fruit consistent with the One who planted it. In the present view, this "seed" is the word of God which produces fruit of God's Spirit (Gal. 5:22–23). Thus, "by this the children of God and the children of the devil are obvious" (3:10): you can tell where a person's true allegiance lies by the fruit (behavior) they produce (Mat. 7:20).

Questions

1.) What does John mean by "the world does not know us" (3:1)? What does this *not* mean?

Why is *purity* (holiness) a critical factor in maintaining our hope of a future life with God (3:3)? What does this purity look like in a Christian's life?

2.) John *separates* the practice of sin from the practice of righteousness (3:7–10). Why is this explanation necessary?

   a. Do you think Christians today are all on the same page regarding this separation of sin and righteousness? Or might some Christians make provision for a "gray area" or things that are "not exactly wrong"? (According to John's epistle, does God recognize any "gray areas" of moral behavior?)

   b. Please read 2 Cor. 6:14–7:1 together with 1 John 3:7–10. What stands out to you as you read these two passages together?

Lesson Five

"Love One Another" (1 John 3:11–24)

One specific behavior to which John now returns is one's love for his "brother" (i.e., fellow believer in the Lord). He begins by stating this negatively: a satanic "child" is one who does not love his brother. Then he restates this positively: one who loves his brother is born of God [implied] (3:11). This message is what "you have heard from the beginning"—"the beginning" here has a different context than the devil having sinned "from the beginning" (recall 3:8). Here, it is a teaching that his reading audience has personally heard; this undoubtedly refers to Jesus' own teaching (John 13:34–35) as well as what the apostles also taught (Rom. 13:8).

Withholding Love Is a Sin Like Murder (3:12–15): "[N]ot as Cain …" (3:12)—see Gen. 4:1–8 for the account of Cain's murder of his brother, Abel.[42] Notice that John does not point to the murder itself, but the motive *behind* it ("for what reason … ?"). Cain's heart was filled with sin—likely, jealousy, arrogance, hatred, and murderous thoughts. The sin in his heart translated to wicked deeds, culminating in murder (Jude 1:11). In contrast, Abel's heart was filled with a desire to honor God, and his deeds naturally conformed to that desire (Heb. 11:4).

Thus, John likens the withholding of love from one's spiritual brother in Christ to Cain's murder of his physical brother. The first reason for this has to do with how God defines sin. He knows what sins exist in the heart before any outward action is committed—even if *no* such action is committed (compare Mat. 5:21–22). John equates withholding one's love for his brother—an act of the heart, regardless of whether it is manifested publicly—as sinful in God's sight.

The second reason has to do with the result of withholding love for one's brother. God's *love* for us translates to Him giving *life* to us (i.e., those who are born of Him); if He did not *love* us (or if He withheld His love from us), we could not be made *alive* in Him through Christ (Eph. 2:4–

5). We who are "children of God" are to imitate this love and therefore extend life to fellow believers by serving their best interests. When we withhold love, we withhold life; even worse, we *rob* our "brother" of the life-giving kindness that God expected us to show to him.[43] Thus, when we withhold love, we act as murderers; in such cases, we no longer walk as righteous Abel, but we emulate his wicked brother, Cain.[44]

"Do not be surprised, brethren, if the world hates you" (3:13). One's practice of godly love elicits hatred, enmity, and even murder from those who refuse to love. A believer ought to be even more surprised if the world *embraced* him and his belief. "The world hates us because it can see the difference between our godly lives and its own evil."[45] Here, John addresses his readers as "brethren"—i.e., instead of giving instruction to them as a father to his children, he regards them as fellow-sufferers, himself being a fellow recipient of the hatred of those who hate Christ.

When we love one another, "we know that we have passed out of death into life" (3:14).[46] This does not mean we are saved *because* we have loved one another, but that the demonstration of our love is consistent with those who are saved. The "brethren" (all Christians) must be the primary object of our love; if we cannot love our spiritual brothers in Christ, then we are unprepared to love those who remain outside of Christ—all sinners, including our enemies (Mat. 5:44). "He who does not love abides in death"—an intentional paradox: he *lives* in *death*. Since he walks in the darkness (and has no fellowship in God's Light), his soul is "dead" to God (Eph. 2:1–3). When love flourishes, life flourishes; when unlovingness reigns, "death" results.

"Everyone who hates his brother is a murderer" (3:15)—whether he kills someone is irrelevant; by refusing to love like God loves, he carries murder in his heart.[47] The withholding of godly love translates to a worldly, hateful, and murderous spirit like that found in Cain's own blackened heart. "[N]o murderer has eternal life abiding in him"—this states one's present condition, not what it could be if such a person believed in Christ, repented of his sins, and called upon the name of the Lord for salvation. But John is not talking about just *any* murderer, but one who professes to be a *Christian* and yet withholds love from his fellow believer. Such a person cannot abide in God or have God abiding in his loveless heart. No one can walk in moral darkness *and* God's Light at the same time.

Love in Action (3:16–18): Now John begins to give definition and dimension to what love for the brethren requires of us (3:16–18). Just as Jesus laid down His life for us (John 15:12–14, Rom. 5:6–8), so we are to lay down *our own* lives for fellow believers. This statement can be taken both literally and figuratively.

- When taken literally—i.e., when we choose to die alongside or to save a fellow brother or sister in Christ—then the implied condition must be "if necessary." We must not choose to be careless with our lives and mistake this for something noble and virtuous; at the same time, we have surrendered controlling interest of our lives to Christ and His church, and we thus accept whatever sacrifices are required to honor this. Christ did not *figuratively* lay down His life for us; He *in fact* died to save us. Our own physical death may be required to serve the greater good of God's heritage.
- When taken figuratively, "[laying] down our lives for the brethren" is unlimited in scope. It seems evident John is contrasting two kinds of death: the hate-filled *murder* of one who will not give his love to the brethren; and the love-filled *sacrifice* of one who loves God and thus loves those who belong to Him. In the first case, it is one of the "brethren" who dies; in the second case, it is the one who *loves* "the brethren" who dies—that is, who gives up himself to serve the best interest of his brother (1 Thess. 2:8).

All godly love is sacrificial in nature. No one can love *like* God without laying down his *own* life just as the Son of God laid down *His* life. Jesus explicitly said that we must love one another as He has loved us—literally (if necessary) and figuratively (in all cases). Actions speak louder than words.

A Christian whom God has abundantly blessed but refuses to let go of such gifts to help a fellow brother in need contradicts this loving spirit (3:17). By closing his heart against his brother, he practices darkness, hatred, and murder rather than light, love, and sacrifice. He will not *literally* lay down his life for this brother in need because he is unwilling even *figuratively* to lay down his life (as represented by his goods or possessions; see Mat. 16:25–26 and Luke 12:15). Laying down your life for the brethren, then, rarely results in death but it must *always* result in letting go of the "world's goods" (i.e., things necessary for life) to help our brother or sister in Christ who is truly in need of these things.[48]

The mere profession of brotherly love ("with word or with tongue") is nothing more than lip service (3:18). Words are cheap and meaningless until accompanied by corresponding action ("in deed and truth"). "Deeds" are visible, historical, and practical demonstrations of love; "truth" indicates the sincere and authentic nature of such deeds. Real love seeks to fulfill the best interests of another person. It is not pretentious, forced, or burdensome, but reflects God's own selfless love for us.

Confidence in God's Grace (3:19–22): By our demonstrations of love in deed and truth—"we will know … that we are of the truth …" (3:19). Those who are taught God's word, led by His Spirit, and conform to the image of His Son, will manifest godly characteristics toward others. When we love the brethren as God has taught us to love them (which requires that we obey His commandments), then this "will assure our heart before Him in whatever our heart condemns us" (3:19b–20a). Our righteous acts of love toward His people makes our standing with God evident. (Obviously, the opposite is also true: if we have *no* such evidence of godly love, then neither can we be in favor with Him.)

John is addressing a common concern among Christians. Even sincere and honest Christians can wonder if they have done enough, or if they are adequately expressing God's love in their lives. Even though we know the right information and are trying hard to fulfill what God expects of us, we still may have doubts concerning our fellowship with Him. It is likely that every single Christian has gone through this conscience-wringing experience in which his heart condemns him despite what the gospel teaches to the contrary. John provides the necessary confirmation that we seek, however, our acts of love and kindness toward God's people is indicative of our good fellowship with God. Such acts are not *instead* of obedience to His commandments but are the visible *results* of such obedience.

"[F]or God is greater than our heart and knows all things" (3:20b)—i.e., our feelings of doubt or inadequacy do not disturb God. He does not *think* we are fulfilling our Christian obligations; He *knows* we are. He does not *hope* we are doing well; He *knows* we are doing well. God's true and accurate knowledge of our heart is far superior to the subjective and emotional appraisal that we might have of it. "[F]or we walk by faith, not by sight" (2 Cor. 5:7), but God dwells in unapproachable Light and operates with infallible Truth.

"[I]f our heart does *not* condemn us, we have confidence before God" (3:21, emphasis added). This cannot mean, "If I feel that what I am doing is right, then I can stand before God with a clear conscience." **First,** no one becomes righteous through a mere "feeling"—whether his own or anyone else's. **Second,** righteousness is something God determines, not us, and no one can be righteous who will not keep His commandments. **Third,** it is God who cleanses the conscience through the blood of Christ (Heb. 9:13–14); nothing else is capable of this. Our good deeds—however many or noble they might be—cannot cleanse a single sin from one's soul.

What John must mean here (in context) is this: those who know God's commandments and know they are doing their best to fulfill them—not perfectly, but *authentically*—can stand with confidence before God's throne. This, not on their own merit (for they have none worthy of such standing), but Christ's. It is "by *His* doing" and not ours that God justifies us (1 Cor. 1:30). Nonetheless, it remains true that we can *know* (by faith) whether we are walking with God in the Light. And if this is so, then we can approach Him with boldness, confidence, and assurance (Heb. 10:19–22).

Our approach to the throne of God allows us to bring our petitions before Him, whether for ourselves or on behalf of others (3:22a; compare Heb. 4:16). Whatever we *ask*, however, we must believe we will *receive*, in whatever form, manner, or time God chooses to fulfill our requests. We dare not ask without faith (James 1:6–8), but faith rests upon evidence and historical action. God's word (and all He has proved *in* His word) is one part of that evidence and action; our acts of love and mercy are another. We can know we will receive (or, be granted) our requests of God "because we keep His commandments and do the things that are pleasing in His sight" (3:22b).

John does not mean that *any* and *every* request will be granted, however. Believers know to make their petitions within the context of God's will (Mat. 6:10, 1 John 5:14). The very motivation for "asking" means we let God make the final decision, and/or allow Him to amend the request as He sees fit, according to His omniscient will. This is also true for other passages that seem at first to invite open-ended requests (John 15:7, 16:23, etc.). The better we learn to keep God's commandments, the better we understand what His will is for us. Through this process, our prayers become increasingly conformed to His will rather than to our own. We ask, He answers; we seek, He reveals; we knock, He opens doors or keeps them shut (Mat. 7:7–8).

What Christ Has Commanded Us (3:23–24): "This is His commandment …" (3:23–24)—the "commandment" is singular, yet the definition is plural (believe *and* love). This is not a contradiction, since these are not two separate commands but one; or, we could say the commands are inseparable from each other and thus must be taken *as* one. To have fellowship with God, confidence to stand before Him, and answers to prayers, one must keep this twofold "commandment."

- **First,** he must believe in what the gospel teaches concerning the true nature and identity of Jesus the Man: He is also the Christ, the Son of God—a Divine Being who stands in relation to the Father as no other being does or can.
- **Second,** he must *obey* the Son, a specific manifestation of this obedience being his love for fellow believers. Only *such* a person will "abide" or dwell in God's presence and will also enjoy the indwelling of God's Spirit. "We know by this that He abides in us"—this "knowing" is an experiential one, not merely a fact-based understanding. "By the Spirit whom He has given us"—the freedom

from condemnation (guilt) through the cleansing of Jesus' blood provides for the indwelling of God's Spirit (2 Cor. 3:17). Thus, if God does cleanse one of his sins, He also blesses him with His Spirit.

So far in this epistle John has linked together actions necessary for the salvation of the believer:

- We have fellowship with the Father when we walk in the Light, are cleansed by the blood of His Son and receive the indwelling of His Spirit.
- "[W]alking in the Light" means that we keep God's commandments, love one another, and abide in His truth.
- When we live in the truth, then we are promised eternal life and will have full confidence of salvation when Jesus returns and brings us to Judgment.
- Living in the truth requires that we practice righteousness and do not practice sin.
- This righteousness requires that we genuinely and actively love those who are also born of God.
- When we live in righteousness and love, then God hears and answers our prayers.

Questions

1.) Why is a Christian who refuses to *give* love to his fellow brother in Christ made equal with a man who selfishly *takes* another person's life (3:15)?

2.) If necessary, Christians are expected to lay down their lives for their brethren (3:16). How does our human nature of self-preservation interfere with this expectation? What are we to *do* about that?

3.) Does John mean (in 3:21) that if we believe in our heart that we are *right*, God will not condemn us? Or does he mean that God will not condemn anyone who is sincere in heart, no matter what he believes? Or what do you think?

Lesson Six

The Spirit of Truth and the Spirit of Error (1 John 4:1–6)

Even though Christians enjoy the indwelling of God's Holy Spirit, there are many other *unholy* spirits that exist. Just as those who claim to "know God" must be tested (recall 2:3–6), so must those who claim to speak for God's Spirit.

Test All Spirits (4:1–3): "[D]o not believe every spirit …" (4:1). These "spirits" are not harmless entities, but desire to manipulate, deceive, and control naïve believers for wicked purposes. They refer to false teachers or prophets—in other words, mere men—but John implies that there is a *sinister* and *demonic* element driving these men.[49] The teaching of these godless, satanic, and worldly "spirits" will not be consistent with what the Holy Spirit has revealed in Christ's gospel. Christians are strongly warned *not* to "believe every spirit" that presents itself as a genuine spokesman for God—which is what the early Christians did (Rev. 2:2).[50]

The standard for this testing is the word of God, as revealed by the Spirit of God to Christ's chosen apostles. Since there is only one gospel—one message of truth (Eph. 1:13, 4:4–6)—any departure from this must be false. "It is significant that it was John's *readers* who were to make the test and not some ecclesiastical dignity or official head."[51] While these false prophets can easily deceive those who have no spiritual grounding in the truth, they must be exposed and repelled by those who *know* the truth and *by* the truth. "[M]any false prophets have gone out into the world," as has always been the case (Mat. 7:15, 1 Tim. 4:1, 2 Peter 2:1, etc.).

The Holy Spirit will not—indeed, *cannot*—speak a lie, and therefore cannot provide a false teaching concerning Jesus (1 Cor. 12:3). Likewise, a person who claims to speak by the authority of God cannot contradict what the Spirit has already revealed through the apostles. "[E]very spirit that confesses that Jesus Christ has come in the flesh is from God"

(4:2)—meaning: to deny this is to deny the prophecies of God, the fact that Christ is the center of all human history, and His kingship. "[H]as come in the flesh" in the Greek indicates He was *born* "in the flesh," and did not mystically indwell an already-existing man. Rather, "the Word became flesh" (John 1:14) and remained "flesh" throughout His entire earthly existence, even in His death.

Those who teach otherwise (as the Gnostics did, one way or another) are "not from God" (4:3), regardless of who they are or how convincing they may be. Instead, "the is the spirit of the antichrist" (recall 2:18, 22). An "antichrist" is not any one person or entity but is the demonic spirit of error and deceit that opposes Christ, His gospel, and His people. John has already predicted the rise of this "spirit" in 2:18 (compare Acts 20:29–30, 1 Tim. 4:1, and 2 Tim. 3:1); now, as John writes, it is already active and attempting to infiltrate the brotherhood.

Consider the Source of Who Is Speaking (4:4–6): While antichrists are servants of Satan, "You [Christians] are from God" and therefore should not be afraid of our opponents (4:4). The power of antichrists is far inferior to God's Spirit ("He who is in you") who indwells believers. "[H]e who is in the world" is not Satan himself, but those who are under his power (see 5:19). Since Christ's ascension to His throne, Satan has been "cast out" from God's presence (as predicted in John 12:31) and "cast down" to the earth (Rev. 12:7–10). He fills the world with lies, deceptions, and moral error, and the "antichrists" have swallowed these and now attempt to sow satanic error among the brotherhood. "They [the antichrists] are from the world" (4:5)—i.e., they derive their power and gratification from the world and its lusts (recall 2:15–16). The "world"—the collective term for the self-serving, carnal-minded, and satanic spirit of men—does not want to listen to those who are born of God. The two groups are in opposition to each other, since they each follow a different spirit (Gal. 5:16–17).

"We are from God" (4:6)—the "we" being a direct reference to the original teachers of the word of God, Christ's own apostles (recall 1:1–3 and comments). Thus, *we* (apostles) have taught the message of divine truth so that *you* (Christians) can have fellowship with God based upon this teaching. "[H]e who knows God" personally is one who (based upon what John has already written) has fellowship with God; walks in the Light; keeps God's commandments; abides in the truth; and loves the brethren. Such a person will listen to the apostolic teaching because of his love for God and His truth.

"[H]e who is not from God" listens to some other god, walks in the darkness, and believes in lies that masquerade as truth. He rejects those who teach the truth because he stands opposed to it. Simply put, the apostles are the true teachers of God; antichrists are false teachers and impostors. "By this"—that is, by comparing the *authority* of the two groups (apostles and antichrists) and the *source* of their teaching (from God or "the world")—Christians can discern what is true from what is false, what is sound teaching from what is false teaching, and what is of God's Spirit from what is of the world's spirit (1 Tim. 6:3–4a, Heb. 5:14).

Questions

1.) God's word commands us to "test" any person who claims to be a prophet of God (4:1). *How* do we "test" such a person? What if, despite failing the test, that person still claims to be a sincere and genuine prophet—what do we do then?

2.) What exactly does "confess Jesus" mean in the context in which John uses this phrase (4:3)? What does it *not* mean?

3.) John says false "spirits" (prophets) speak as though "from the world" (4:5). What does he mean by this? How is this different from how Christians are supposed to speak? (Consider Mat. 5:37, Eph. 5:4, Col. 4:6, and 1 Peter 4:11 in your answer.)

Lesson Seven

"God Is Love"
(1 John 4:7–21)

"**God Is Love**" (**4:7–10**): What John says in these verses about godly love is as important to us as Paul's own discourse on love in 1 Cor. 13. He begins with an earnest plea to "love one another," but immediately provides the reason for this: "for love is from God" (4:7).[52] Love [Greek, *agape*] is the supreme attribute of God's nature, since everything He does is motivated by His love and serves the best interest of those who are loved by Him. Likewise, this must be the supreme attribute of those who are "born of God," and that which motivates everything *we* do and serves the best interests of those whom *we* love. It is impossible to "know" God yet refuse to obey His commandment to love and imitate His own holy nature.[53]

"God is love" (4:8b) does *not* mean "God is a *loving* God"; "Love is one of God's finest characteristics"; "God is full of love"; or "Love is God." Rather, John speaks of God's essential nature: He is not a God *of* love, but He *is* love. Love is not something God thinks about (as a virtuous sentiment), radiates (as a positive influence), or does (as a noble action); love is *what God is all about*. This means He cannot *withhold* love, "for He cannot deny Himself" (2 Tim. 2:13). Whatever He thinks, radiates, or does is an expression of who He is.

It is common for people to impose upon God their own *version* or *expectations* of love (such as, "How can a loving God allow evil in the world?"), but such assessments only focus on what they think a so-called "loving God" might *do*, not who God really *is*. Because God *is* love, He never ceases to *act* in love, regardless of whether we fully understand those actions.

The finest expression of God's essential nature—His love—is in His having given His Son to be an atoning sacrifice for our sins (4:9). Through this unprecedented and completely undeserved action, His love was "manifested in [or, toward] us." Because Christians have been *saved* through and then *transformed* by His love, we can testify to the selfless and genuine demonstration of divine love He provided through the cross. The reason for Christ having "appeared" (recall 3:5) is "so that we might live through Him" (4:9).

God does not love us because we first loved Him, but quite the opposite: we love *Him* because He first loved *us* (4:10). As Paul said, "While we were yet sinners"—i.e., before and even regardless of whether we loved God in return—"Christ died for us" (Rom. 5:8). The order of who acted *first* in securing our salvation is consistent throughout the NT. On "propitiation," see comments on 2:2.

"Love One Another" (4:11–12): "Beloved, if God so loved us …" (4:11)—in this context, "if" means "since," for it is abundantly clear throughout the NT that God *does* "so love" us (recall 3:1). Given this irrefutable truth, the giving of His Son being its ultimate proof, "we also ought to love one another." It is impossible for us to demonstrate properly our love for God unless or until we demonstrate godly love toward one another. "One another," in this context, specifically refers to those who are born of God (see 5:1–2). While Christ instructs Christians to love *all* people, including our enemies (Mat. 5:44), we cannot show the full expression of our love to those who remain outside of Christ's community of believers (His church). Yet, we are "especially" to love fellow Christians, since we *all* are joined together in Christ (Gal. 6:10).

God's love—its quality, virtue, application, and unconditional offering—provides the ideal and only acceptable model for what we call "godly love." Any form of love that is *less* or *different* than His love is not "godly love," regardless of what one says otherwise. Likewise, no love can be "godly love" that fails to honor God and/or His people. "[W]e also ought to love one another" (4:11)—i.e., this is the behavior expected of us even when we fail to practice it. Reasons for this include: we have an excellent Example (in the Father's love); we have an excellent Teacher (in Christ's own life); we have excellent reinforcement (in the apostolic teaching on this subject); we have excellent opportunities (in the brotherhood); and we have no *good* reason to refuse to do this.

"No one has seen God at any time" (4:12)—*but* when we love one another, people do (in essence) "see" God in us (Mat. 5:16). Our habitual, selfless, and unconditional love for one another is evidence that "God abides in us" or indwells our hearts. No one can love like God loves who is not first born of Him *and* transformed by His divine love. "His love is perfected in us" means the love He has shown *toward* us is gradually and experientially maturing *in* us as we draw near to Him and practice what He has taught us.

We Abide in God, God Abides in Us (4:13–17): Further evidence that God "abides" (lives, dwells, or is present) in us is in our having received His Spirit (4:13). This reception began at our water baptism into Christ (Acts 2:38) in which we were "washed," "justified," and "sanctified" by Christ's authority and "in the Spirit of our God" (1 Cor. 6:11). Wherever God the Father is, so must be His Spirit (and vice versa); if God indwells faithful Christians, then so must His Spirit (Rom. 8:9).

John's instructions here have nothing to do with the abiding of God's Spirit within us for the purpose of performing miracles; the present context is general, practical, and universal among all genuine believers (which is not the case for spiritual gifts). John's point here is to reaffirm that the entire Godhead—the Father, Son, and Holy Spirit—are intimately and profoundly involved in the salvation of every Christian *since* that person strives to practice those things which he (or she) has learned from the Godhead.

John again ties together the apostles' testimony of Christ's divine nature and one's fellowship with God the Father (recall 1:1–4). "We have seen and testify" (4:14a) describes eyewitnesses (John and other apostles), not those who came after (i.e., the rest of us). You and I did not see Christ, His miracles, or His resurrected self; our testimony about His divine nature is all based upon what the apostles saw and recorded for us. The Father did not just *say* He sent His Son into the world; He *proved* it, and the apostles *saw* these proofs.

"Savior of the world" (4:14b) indicates a universal *call* to sinners everywhere (a biblical teaching), not an automatic *saving* of every person (a human doctrine called "universalism"). God calls people through His gospel, which is available to all men through the work of His Spirit (2 Thess. 2:13–14). Because of apostolic testimony concerning Jesus' divine nature, we can know for certain that He is "the Son of God" (4:15). To "confess" this is to speak and live in agreement with this truth; it is to say (in words and deeds) the same thing God has said.[54] It is impossible to be in fellowship with God without agreeing that Christ is Lord and submitting to His authority. Thus, of the one who so speaks and so lives, "God abides in him, and he in God."

In 4:16–17, John summarizes what he has just said and transitions into the next thought: "We know God loves us—this has been established; when we love like He loves, then we have nothing to fear after death" (my paraphrase). "God is love," and His love conditions and governs those who live to Him; this governance prepares us for our presentation before Him in the hereafter. "Confidence" is a repeating topic in John's epistle, as it is throughout the entire NT.[55] Since God has given us every reason to *believe* in Him, He wants His people to be *confident* about their faith. Lack of belief leads to a lack of confidence; lack of confidence leads to an ineffective and unproductive "Christian" lifestyle.

The "day of judgment" (4:17) will be a terrifying and awful experience for those who were never in Christ or who once believed but did not remain committed to that belief (2 Thess. 1:6–9, Rev. 20:11–15). However, it will be a day of glory, vindication, and inexpressible joy for those who walked with God in this life, for they shall surely walk with God forever in the life to come. "[A]s He is, so also are we in this world"—as we have embraced His love, adopted His will as our own, and conformed to His holy nature, so we identify with Him *now* and will always be with Him in the *hereafter*.

Love Casts Out Fear (4:18–21): "There is no fear in love …" (4:18), where "in love" refers to the safeguarding of the Father's love for those who obey His commandments. This cannot mean such people (Christians) are fearless; it means *in the Judgment* they have nothing to fear. "[P]erfect love casts out fear"—i.e., embracing God's love *and* imitating that love in one's own behavior dispels all worries about what is to come in the hereafter. The fear of death (and the judgment and punishment that follows) fills the unbeliever's heart with dread, and rightly so.

But God is not going to punish the one who has entrusted his soul to His care; God does not punish the innocent or those *made* innocent through the blood of His Son (recall 1:7, 9). "Perfect love" cannot mean flawless love, because only God is capable of this; it refers instead to a mature, goal-oriented, and active love as expressed through a joyful keeping of God's commandments.[56] The reception of divine love prepares one's soul for his presentation before God; in the absence of this reception, a person's heart has only spiritual torment and "a terrifying expectation of judgment" (Heb. 10:27) rather than peace and confidence. "It is self-interested love that fears; pure and unselfish love has no fear."[57]

"We love, because He first loved us" (4:19). This does not say, "We love *God*, because … ," but simply, "We *love*, because … ." All expressions of godly love, including our love for God, are in response to and a reflection of His love. We did not invent this love; it did not originate with us; we did not teach God how to love *us*, but He taught us how to love Him, others, and ourselves. Therefore, "If someone says, 'I love God,' and hates his brother, he is a liar" (4:20), since he is not truly practicing the love of the Father. God loves *all* people, and especially those who are "in Christ" (because of the special relationship they have with Him).

One who claims to love God but withholds love for his brother in the Lord—the essential meaning of "hate" in this case—betrays his love for God and "[lies] against the truth" of his true condition (compare James 3:14). In this case, one's professed love for God (whom he has never seen) is negated by his failure to love his brother (who stands right in front of him). By implication, it is impossible for one's love for God to be authentic who does not actually practice that love toward His people. Once we commit ourselves to loving God (by accepting the terms of His salvation), we commit ourselves also to loving our "brother" in the Lord who also has committed himself to God. This is a command, not an option (4:21). To *like* (or choose to be friends with) someone is a personal choice; to *love* them is a divine command.

Questions

1.) When John says that "everyone who loves is born of God and knows God" (4:7), does he mean that any person's act or version of love necessarily implies his fellowship with God? Why or why not?

2.) If *we* love God and His people according to His gospel, can we *also* "have confidence in the day of judgment" (4:17)?

   a. Does this mean we do not have to worry about keeping His commandments, as long as we love people?

   b. Does this mean those who do *not* love (either God or His people) will be lost, even if they may keep other commandments of God?

3.) Given all that John (and the entire gospel of Christ) has said about "love," how important should this subject be in our present teaching, personal behavior, and congregations? Is this a subject that we should often talk about and strive to understand better? Is it a subject that *you* should be concerned about?

Lesson Eight

Jesus Is the Christ, the Son of God (1 John 5:1–12)

Love and Obedience Go Together (5:1–3): Our love for fellow believers is a necessary extension of our love for God Himself. John defines a Christian as "Whoever believes that Jesus is the Christ is born of God" (5:1). To "believe" here is not mere intellectual consent ("I agree with this statement"), but obedience to what the statement necessarily implies and requires of a person ("Since I believe this, I will live accordingly"). Being "born of God" indicates one's profound change in allegiance: he no longer lives for the world (sinful flesh) but to God (recall 2:29; see Rom. 6:3–10).

"Jesus is the Christ" links Jesus the *Man* (a real, historical, flesh-and-blood person) with Christ the *Son of God* (a real, supra-historical, and divine Personage). The same Person fulfills both roles; to "believe" in His one role requires "believing" in the other, as it is impossible to separate Jesus from "the Christ." In other words, it is impossible for a person to be "born of God" or even "of God" who *denies* that Jesus the Man is indeed Christ the Son of God. And " … whoever loves the Father loves the child born of Him," since all Christians are themselves "sons of God through faith in Christ Jesus" (Gal. 3:26). Thus, to recognize Jesus' Sonship to the Father requires recognition of our fellow believer's "sonship" as well.

John circles back to what he stated earlier (in 2:3–6), but with reversed emphasis. Instead of saying, "If we love God, then we must love Christians also," he says here (5:2), in essence, "The only proper way to love Christians is to love God and keep His commandments." "We know" here involves a conscious understanding or awareness of what is real and true. One cannot *know* God who is not living *truthfully* to His commandments. Despite modern resistance to or avoidance of doctrine, commandments, and authority, John is direct and unapologetic: keeping God's commandments is necessary to love Him (5:3a). This means that one who refuses (for any reason) to keep God's commandments also betrays his professed love for the Father.

"His commandments are not burdensome" (5:3b) means that God does not intend to burden or oppress us with them; rather, He gives these for our benefit. God's commandments *seem* burdensome only when we resist or try to evade them; and the difficulty of keeping His commandments pales in comparison to the difficulty of trying to save ourselves against all hope (Mat. 11:28–30).

Sometimes Christians make God's commandments more difficult than they really are simply by adding to them our own commentary, expectations, or traditional misunderstandings. In such cases, we burden ourselves with something that did not come from God, but that we *think* came from Him. "Not burdensome" does not mean "easy," but *doable* through the strength which God supplies. "His commandments are not a burden but a privilege and an opportunity to show our love."[58]

Faith Overcomes the World (5:4–5): Being "born of God" incurs a profound responsibility, yet what the born-again believer receives from God is far greater than whatever he gives to Him. While keeping His commandments is difficult, and may challenge us to our core, our faithful allegiance to Christ will finally win over this struggle (5:4). To "overcome the world" means to prevail against all the world forces of sin and corruption that tried to destroy us in the first place (1 Peter 1:3–9). To overcome is to be victorious in Christ (Rom. 8:33–37); to *be* overcome is to succumb to evil and be destroyed because of it (Rom. 12:21).

It is not faith *alone* that overcomes the world, nor any *kind* of faith, but faith in Jesus Christ and only the kind of faith He authorizes and then perfects in us (Heb. 12:2). "Who is the one … ?" (5:5)—i.e., a person must believe that Jesus is the Christ to be "born of God"; the result of this spiritual rebirth is that same person's ability to overcome the world *through* Christ.

God's Testimony of His Son (5:6–12): Jesus Christ "is the One who came by water and blood …" (5:6). Some believe the "water and the blood" refers to what John witnessed when the soldier pierced Jesus' side after He had died (John 19:34).[59] But the present text (5:1–8) gives no reason to connect with that event. The only thing that blood and water from His side proved is that Jesus was genuinely dead; it does not prove He was the Christ.

There is no logical point of reference for John's statement (in 5:6) except in Christ's actual earthly ministry. His ministry began with water (His baptism—Mat. 3:13–17) and ended with blood (in His death, the "blood of His cross"—Col. 1:20). This is how He "came" to us—i.e., how He presented Himself to the world in His ministry. Certain Gnostics believed that Christ (the divine Son of God) was indeed "in" Jesus the Man during His ministry but departed from Him before His crucifixion. They believed that God's holiness could have no association with death and shame; thus, Jesus the Man died on the cross, but not Christ the Son of God.

Yet from the beginning to the end of Jesus' ministry, as bookmarked by the water of His baptism and the blood of His cross, there was no change in His nature. In fact, not only do the water and blood provide testimony to the dual nature of Jesus, but so does the Holy Spirit (5:7–8; see John 16:7–11). The Spirit bears witness to the truth of Jesus' dual nature (as a human *and* divine being) and the legitimacy of His ministry (see John 3:31–35, for example).

" … [A]nd the three [water, blood, and Spirit] are in agreement" (5:8b)—i.e., they all witness the same truth, and lead to the same inescapable conclusion: Jesus the Man *is* Christ the Son of God. Some later biblical manuscripts include (immediately after the words of 5:7, "There are three that testify") " … in heaven, the Father, the Word, and the Holy Spirit, and these are one. And there are three that testify on earth …"—leading into 5:8, " … the Spirit and the water and the blood …" However, there is no good reason to accept this insertion as genuine.

The "testimony of men" (5:9) is susceptible to misunderstandings, errors, and conflicts of interest. And yet, people will receive human testimony to determine spiritual truths. Such "testimony" is of the earth, not of heaven; it lacks authority, authenticity, and proof. The "testimony of God," however, transcends the limitations and errors of men; it has legitimate authority, authenticity, and proof (John 5:33, 37, 8:18, 12:27–30, etc.). This "testimony" is provided specifically in the water, blood, and Spirit of Jesus' earthly ministry, and generally in all the other heavenly proofs that conclude the same thing (John 5:30–47).

Those who accept God's testimony agree with Him and have the indwelling of His Spirit; thus, they have "the testimony in [themselves]" (5:10; see Rom. 8:9, 16). One who rejects God's testimony (and receives the testimony of men instead) "has made Him a liar"—not in fact, but accusatorily (recall 1:10). The irony is that such men (who insinuate that God's testimony is wrong or insufficient) also seek His salvation. Having rejected Jesus as the Son of God, however, they also reject fellowship with the Father (John 16:2–3). The testimony God provides *concerning* His Son is that believers receive eternal life *through* the Son (5:11; see also John 3:16, 6:40, 17:3, Titus 2:11–14, etc.).

John makes it clear: the Son and "the life" (i.e., eternal life with God) are inseparable (5:12). There can be no other source of life but Him; no one can have "the life" apart from Him ("for apart from Me you can do nothing"—John 15:5). "[H]as the Son" goes both ways: He abides in us, and we are His possession (1 Cor. 6:19–20); as we have *Him*, so He has *us*.

Questions

1.) Why does John say God's commandments "are not burdensome" (5:3) when in fact Jesus said that discipleship to Him is a life-long, cross-bearing, and sacrificial ministry (e.g., Mat. 16:24, Luke 14:26–27)?

2.) In what *way* does our faith "overcome the world" (5:4)? In other words, what is it about our faith in God that allows us to prevail against the temptations, resistance, and false religion of the world?

3.) John says, "If we receive the testimony of men, the testimony of God is greater" (5:9). Despite all the evidence God has provided concerning His Son (and His Son's reign over all the world), why do so many people refuse to accept this testimony and choose instead to listen to men and man-made religion?

4.) What does it mean to "have the Son" regarding salvation (5:12)? Can one be mistaken about whether he has the Son? Please explain.

Lesson Nine
Praying with Confidence (1 John 5:13–21)

Requests Made According to His Will (5:13–15): "These things have been written … so that you may know that you have eternal life" (5:13). To "know" here means to have understanding, awareness, and realization (of something).[60] Thus, whether we have (or, from our present perspective, can anticipate) eternal life is not a mysterious or unknowable thing. Just as John wrote his gospel account so people "may believe that Jesus is the Christ, the Son of God; and that believing you may have life in His name" (John 20:31), so he has written this epistle. Once a person is confident that he stands in a favorable relationship with God, and he can rightfully anticipate eternal life with Him, he can be filled with joy (recall 1:4).

As we have confidence in eternal life with God, so we can have confidence in the prayers we submit to Him (5:14–15). "[I]f we ask anything according to His will, He hears us" means:

- We need (and are expected) to *ask God* for whatever we presently lack or that we believe needs to continue. Jesus instructed us to "ask," "seek," and "knock" in prayerful pursuit of God's help (Mat. 7:7–8). If we do not petition God, if we ask without believing (James 1:6–8, 4:2), or if we ask with the wrong motives (James 4:3), then we should not expect to receive anything from Him. However, if we *do* ask and *do* believe and *do* have the right motives, God will supply us with everything we need (Luke 11:1–13).
- "according to His will" conditions all our requests. Jesus said, "If you abide in Me, and My words abide in you, ask whatever you wish, and it will be done for you" (John 15:7). But we must keep such statements in the context of all other NT teachings on prayer. Neither John nor Jesus is saying that prayer is a self-generated "wish list" that God is obligated to fulfill. Rather, the full implication is that whatever a believer in Christ asks of God must be within the

context of His will. Even in cases when we do not *know* His exact will on a given matter (e.g., whether He wants a "door" to be opened or closed; whether He wants a sick person to be healed; whether He wants to grant our request or deny it; etc.), still our prayers are to be fully subject to His will. In other words, we can ask for whatever we want, but we should never knowingly ask for something that contradicts His will. In any case, God must always have the final say—**first**, because He is God; and **second**, because we *give Him this right* when we humbly offer our petitions to Him.

❏ "He hears us"—i.e., *when* we ask, He *does* listen and *will* respond. How, when, and in whatever measure He chooses to respond is up to Him; the fact remains, however, that He will indeed give us an answer, even if the answer is "no" or "wait." Thus, we "must ask in faith without any doubting" (James 1:6). God already knows what we need (Mat. 6:8), but He wants us to demonstrate faith and confidence in Him by laying our petitions at His feet (1 Peter 5:7). Because we know He hears us, we can also know our requests to Him will not be in vain.

Situations We *Can* (and *Cannot*) Pray for (5:16–17): John then gives us an example of what *is* "according to His will" and what is *not*. We can offer prayers on behalf of a "brother"—i.e., a fellow Christian—"committing a sin not {leading} to death" (5:16). On the other hand, we must never petition God to forgive sins that *do* lead to death. While there are other difficult passages in John's epistle, this is one of the most difficult of them all. (John's original reading audience may have had a clearer understanding of what John is talking about than we do.)

Upon first reading, this passage seems to say that some sins are not as bad as others. It is far more accurate to say that John refers to one's *attitude* toward sin rather than categorizing sins according to their severity. We can petition God's forgiveness on behalf of one who is not *practicing* sin but simply commits an act he knows is wrong. By implication, this person takes responsibility for this sin by confessing it, repenting of it, and then personally asking for forgiveness (recall 1:7, 9). One's petition on this brother's behalf is not *instead* of this but is *supportive* of it (as in James 5:15–16). This petition is meant to lend confidence to the "brother" who has sinned (and who may have requested this help himself) rather than to convince God to forgive him.

Some see in this passage an indirect response to Gnosticism. Certain Gnostics believed that sins committed in the flesh were inconsequential to one's spiritual standing with God. Since (they taught) the mortal body had no effect on the spiritual soul, one could indulge in immorality and other sins without incurring divine judgment. In response to this, John is saying, "You cannot petition God to forgive someone who does not believe his sin to be real, condemned, and punishable" (recall 1:8, 10). The "sin {leading} to death," in this case, is the refusal to believe that Jesus is the Christ, the Son of God. Such refusal negates all appeals for God's forgiveness; furthermore, it leads to behavior that violates Christ's holy nature.

"All unrighteousness is sin, and there is a sin not {leading} to death" (5:17). John has already stated (in 3:4–9) that:

- God forbids any chronic and impenitent practice of sin.
- "sin is lawlessness," meaning, *all* sin is a violation of God's laws (or, His holy nature).
- it is impossible to reconcile the practice of sin and fellowship with God.
- those who practice righteousness must conform to Christ's own holy life.
- those who practice sin conform to "the devil," not Christ.
- those "born of God" cannot practice sin, since this betrays their new (spiritual) birth.

Given John's apostolic authority, whatever he says in 5:16–17 cannot contradict what he said in 3:4–9. Those born of God (i.e., Christians) who sin against God have spiritual recourse through the blood of Christ (recall 2:1–2). However, those who will not repent of their sin(s) cannot petition God for forgiveness—nor can anyone petition Him on their behalf—because they have not satisfied the requirements for this petition. Likewise, those who refuse to believe that Jesus the Man is also Christ the Son of God cannot petition God for forgiveness—nor can anyone petition Him on their behalf—because they have rejected the source *of* forgiveness, namely, the blood of God's Son that was shed upon the cross.

"All unrighteousness is sin" (5:17)—*all* sin is a violation of God's holiness and therefore must be dealt with in a responsible manner. However, there *are* sins for which there is no recourse:

- **Speaking against (or, blasphemy of) the Holy Spirit** (Mat. 12:31–32). This *specifically* refers to eyewitnesses of Jesus' miracles—all performed by the power of the Holy Spirit—who refused to believe in the Spirit's testimony (Mat. 12:22–29 and John 16:8–11). This also applies to all people who read the record of Jesus' miracles in the gospel accounts and yet persistently refuse to believe in Him because of these works (John 10:25, 37–38, and 15:24). No one can receive forgiveness of sins who rejects the divine power and authority that testifies to it, namely, the miraculous testimony of the Holy Spirit. While all this is true, there is no reason to think John refers to this situation, but to either of the next two possibilities instead.
- **Rejecting the divine nature of Jesus.** A primary purpose of John's epistle has been to declare that Jesus *is* the Christ. This necessarily means that Jesus the Man is also the divine Being who came from the Father and now intercedes for those who are "born of God." Rejection of this fact prevents forgiveness of sins, fellowship with God, and confidence in the day of judgment. God cannot save anyone who refuses to believe in the Savior whom He sent.
- **Impenitence, or the chronic practice of sin.** Those who will not repent of their sins cannot come to God for spiritual healing and eternal life, since they will not comply with the essential premise of the gospel (Luke 13:3, 5, 24:46–47, Acts 2:38, 3:19, etc.). Those who once made a commitment to follow Christ but refuse to repent of their sins forfeit the salvation that they once sought. Those who fall away from their commitment altogether (in a complete rejection of His grace) also forfeit eternal life with God, and "it is impossible to renew them again to repentance" (Heb. 6:6). This thought supports

what John has repeatedly said about those who practice sin rather than righteousness.

Christians are to be holy in all our behavior; we must not conform to the world (Rom. 12:1–2, 1 Peter 1:13–16). We must not be looking for ways to justify sin, nor can we be lax or delinquent in taking care of our sins. John's appeal is forthright and unapologetic; it also serves our best interest and keeps us close to God's heart. This is not only where we *need* to be to enjoy the fullness of spiritual life with Him, but also where we should *want* to be out of gratitude for what He has done for us through His Son, Jesus Christ.

God's Protection for Those Born of Him (5:18–21): The next verse (5:18) requires close attention: "We know that no one who is born of God sins; but He who was born of God keeps him, and the evil one does not touch him."

- ❑ **First,** there is a change in the verb tense from "is born" to "was born"; this indicates two different people are being addressed. John has consistently referred to one who *is* born of God (present tense) as one who believes in Jesus Christ (recall 2:29, 3:9, 4:7, 5:1, and 5:4). The one who *was* born of God (past tense) must refer to someone else, and there is only one possibility: the only "begotten" of the Father (John 1:14, 3:16, etc.). Thus, Christ "keeps" (i.e., guards, watches over, or protects) him through His divine intercession made on the believer's behalf.
- ❑ **Second,** "the evil one does not touch him" indicates that Christ's protection of the believer is far more powerful than the wicked efforts of the "evil one" to sabotage his faith. There is no reason to believe "the evil one" is anyone other than Satan, whom John earlier called "the devil" (recall 3:8). Christ allows Satan to tempt the believer, but only so far and only with so much; he cannot tempt him beyond what he is able to endure (again, 1 Cor. 10:13). Satan can accuse the believer before God, but he cannot condemn the one whom God has justified through the blood of His Son (Rom. 8:33).

"We know that we are of God" (5:19a) if indeed we believe Jesus is the Christ; obey His commandments; appeal to Christ for forgiveness when we do sin. Such is a summary of what John has already covered in this epistle. We also know "the whole world lies in {the power} of the evil one" (5:19b).[61] This is *not* because Satan has overtaken the world with sovereign power and divine authority, for he does not possess such authority and is not a divine being. He has power over "the world"—in this context, the secular domain of unconverted people—only because "the world" has entrusted him with its own power and attention.

One final thing we "know" (or can understand): "the Son of God has come" (5:20). While the Gnostics inflated themselves with esoteric knowledge and wild imaginations, John points to the absolute certainty of our fellowship with God: the real and living Savior. Jesus "has come"—His coming to earth was an historical, flesh-and-blood reality (John 6:38). Just as we are real, so He was real upon this earth; just as He lived in fellowship with the Father, so we who are born of God live in fellowship with Him. Furthermore, He "has given us understanding" about the Father—understanding that no one else could have provided (John 1:18). He has not only seen the Father in His glory, but the Father showed the Son all that He (the Father) was doing (John 5:19–20).

With such information, "we may know Him who is true"—i.e., the Father Himself.[62] Not only this, but we can know with certainty that we are "in" Him and He is "in" us. While this is a spiritual indwelling (through the Holy Spirit—Rom. 8:9), it is real and effective all the same. When we are "in" the Father, we are also "in" the Son. It is impossible to have fellowship with the Father without also having fellowship with His Son, and vice versa.

"This [lit., this one, just named[63]] is the true God and eternal life" (5:20, referring to Jesus). John states adamantly and affirmatively that Jesus = the Christ = the Son of God. Jesus is a Divine Being who appeared to us as a literal, historical, flesh-and-blood Man (John 1:1–2, Titus 2:13, etc.). He had to come to us in this form to provide the Father with a suitable atonement offering on our behalf (Rom. 8:3–4, Heb. 2:17).

"Little children, guard [or, keep] yourselves from idols" (5:21). This seems at first to be an odd or obscure way of ending this remarkable epistle, yet it is most appropriate. John has spent this entire epistle affirming and confirming the deity of Jesus and has explained that acceptance of His deity is critical to our salvation (recall 2:22–23, 4:15, and 5:1). To believe in anything *less* than this is idolatry; to believe in anyone *other* than Jesus is also idolatry. Idolatry is not the mere bowing down to an image or shrine; it is the worship of *anything* other than God. It is, therefore:

- **misplaced worship.** While only divine Beings (the Father, Son, and Holy Spirit) are deserving of worship, idolaters worship the creation rather than the Creator (Rom. 1:21–25).
- **pride-based worship.** Idolatry is all about giving human power to something inferior to God yet calling that thing "god" and "deliverer" (as ridiculed in Isa. 44:9–20). It is based upon a human decision to *choose* one's "savior" apart from any divine proofs, instructions, or approval—and despite all divine warnings against this.
- **hopeless worship.** Nothing good comes from idolatry. No idol has ever helped or saved anyone. Every person who trusts in an idol (of any kind) for salvation will lose his soul on the Day of Judgment. The idol cannot speak for itself, prescribe good behavior, forgive sins, or provide peace "which surpasses all comprehension" (Phil. 4:7). Whatever the idol "says" is simply an expression of the human heart, like a ventriloquist giving his voice to a dummy. Thus, believing in an idol changes nothing—not one's present circumstances, his sinful condition, or his future.

The Gnostics claimed to believe in God, but they idolized their allegedly special knowledge rather than worship the "Son of God's love" (Col. 1:13), just as the Jews had idolized their temple rather than obeying the One it was built to honor (Jer. 7:3–11). John is warning his Christian readers not to succumb to such elitist folly, despite how intellectually gratifying it might seem.

Those who practice idolatry are not content to keep their false religion to themselves but want to impose it upon others as well. This is all part of their egotistic power trip: despite the fact they know what they are doing is wrong, they encourage others to join them (Rom. 1:18–20, 32). We see this happening repeatedly in the world today.

Questions

1.) John declares that we can *know* we have eternal life (5:13). Yet so many Christians wrangle with self-doubt, fears about death and the Judgment to come, and their own standing with God.

   a. How can we know we have eternal life?

   b. Why should we take comfort in this knowledge?

   c. What are we supposed to *do* with this knowledge—i.e., how should we put this "confidence" in eternal life with God to work?

2.) We know God "hears us in whatever we ask" (5:15), yet He retains the final decision as to when, how, and/or *if* He will fulfill our specific request (or will modify it according to what He knows it best).

   a. Does this mean praying to God is useless, since He is just going to do whatever He wants to do anyway?

b. Or does this mean He *hears* our prayer, but does not really *listen* to what we ask for unless it fits perfectly with what He wanted to do in the first place?

c. Or does this mean prayer should be a finger-crossing, final effort to get God involved in whatever has proved to be too much for us to manage on our own?

d. Or, what do you think?

3.) Since we have surpassed the ancient world in knowledge, historical perspective, technology, and science, is John's warning to "guard yourselves from idols" irrelevant to us today? Why or why not?

Introduction to *2 John* and *3 John*

While often overlooked for their brevity and general lack of theological content, *2 John* and *3 John* reveal a valuable glimpse into the personal correspondence between Christians in the ancient world. "The very shortness of these letters," William Barclay notes, "is the best guarantee of their genuineness. They are so brief and so comparatively unimportant that no one would have gone to the trouble of inventing them and of attaching them to the name of John."[64] Bruce says, "The second and third Epistles of John present us with the closest approximations in the New Testament to the conventional letter-form of the contemporary Graeco-Roman world."[65] In other words, these are excellent examples of ancient letters, regardless of their religious context.

There is hardly any doubt among Bible scholars that the apostle John is the author of both letters.[66] And it is likely that John wrote *2 John* and *3 John* on the same occasion. It is also possible that these letters were sent to the same group (congregation)—one, to the group itself; the other, to a man (Gaius) within the group.[67] The date of writing is unknown, but is most likely concurrent with *1 John*, namely, in the late first century (ca. AD 90–95). We can only guess that both were written from Ephesus, where John resided near the end of his life.

The first centuries of the church did not see a universal acceptance of the canonicity (or New Testament [NT] worthiness) of these two epistles. Often, this was due to their brevity and lack of theological contribution to NT doctrine. Since they were rarely read, rarely quoted or cited, and written to individuals (assuming "the chosen lady" of 2 John *was* an individual; see notes below), they were regarded with suspicion.

On the other hand, they *were* quoted (albeit far less than other books or epistles); they *were* traced back to John by those contemporary with him; and *other* epistles (*1 & 2 Timothy*, *Titus*, and *Philemon*) were also written to individuals and yet deemed canonical. In time, after intense review, they were accepted as part of the NT canon. We must also remember that the same Holy Spirit that inspired men to write such books or letters also oversaw their preservation and their insertion into that body of work we call "the New Testament."

The background of *2 John* and *3 John* is like that of *1 John*: false teaching (particularly, Gnosticism) has infiltrated some churches, and John's letter serves as a warning against and a prescription to avoid this. (On Gnosticism, see "Introduction to *1 John*.") Some churches are doing well in combating this heresy; others, not so well. John has a responsibility as the last surviving apostle of Christ to address problems in the churches but also to encourage those who are striving to do what is right.

In both epistles, there are contrasts between those who "know the truth" and are "walking in truth" (2 John 1:4, 3 John 1:3), such as "the chosen lady and her children," Gaius, and Demetrius; and those who are "deceivers," "antichrists," and men who are so full of themselves that they will not listen to apostolic instruction, such as Gnostic teachers and Diotrephes (2 John 1:7, 3 John 1:9). These letters "reveal that all was not always harmonious, even in the apostolic age, and that human nature, in its darker forms, carried over into the church, and influenced the actions of men even as now. They contain warnings sorely needed in our time, and which should not be ignored or disregarded."[68]

Whereas *1 John* is addressed to no specific group of people other than "my little children" (Christians), *2 John* is addressed to "the chosen lady and her children" (1:1). "Lady" is from the Greek word *kuria* and suggests a proper name (Cyria or Kyria); for this reason, some think this is an actual woman to whom John is writing. Given the context, it seems more appropriate that a congregation is the recipient of this epistle. Speaking to a recipient in the third person would be a very impersonal way to address a known individual but is entirely appropriate for addressing a group of people (a "corporate personality"[69]). Also, personal details of this "lady" are absent from this letter, unlike what we see with John's reference to Gaius in his third epistle.

If this interpretation is accurate, then "lady" is an affectionate way of addressing the leadership of this church—a leadership which is subordinate to its Head (Christ), thus explaining the feminine reference

(Eph. 5:23–24). Her "children," then, refers to faithful members of that congregation. "To speak of a church under the figure of a 'Lady and her Children' is in no sense unlikely and it is probably in this sense such an address was used by the writer."[70] It will be the position of this study to regard this "lady" and "her children" in this way, rather than as an actual person and her biological children.

Third John is addressed to a man named Gaius [pronounced *guy-ee*-us]. All obscure references are dropped because now John is writing to a friend instead of a group of people; this is a private letter, whereas *2 John* is a publicly read letter. Even so, the identity of Gaius remains unknown to us except for what is written in *3 John*. There are four different men named Gaius in the NT.[71] Given the later date in which this epistle was written, and no other correlation between the men named Gaius whom Paul knew and this man whom John knows, there is no good reason to assume *this* Gaius is one of the other Gaius' in the NT.

There are three distinct individuals mentioned in this third epistle: Gaius, Diotrephes, and Demetrius. Two of these men are humble servants to the church whom John commends for exemplary behavior. The third, Diotrephes, is a proud and controlling man who sees fit not only to dispose of fellow Christians, but also to stand opposed to the apostle John himself. "We cannot ascertain where Gaius, Diotrephes, and Demetrius resided. Their place of residence was within traveling distance from Ephesus, so that John in his old age was still able to visit them. Perhaps all we can say is that these people lived in Asia Minor."[72]

Lesson Ten
The Second Epistle of John
(2 John)

Salutation and Introduction (1:1–3): "The elder [or, presbyter] …" (1:1a)—there is no need for John to identify himself as "the apostle," because everyone knows he is one, especially the recipients of this personal letter. Such a title suggests age, veneration, wisdom, respect, and authority; whether John adopted this title himself or was given it is unclear (and irrelevant). He is also not "an" elder, but *the* elder; he is not an elder of a given church, but an elder (in his authoritative position as an apostle of Christ) over *all* the churches. If John is indeed the last surviving apostle, then there is no one else with equal position or authority left on earth.

"Chosen [or, elect; choice] lady" (1:1a)—see "Introduction to *2 John* and *3 John*," where it is determined (for this study) that this "lady" is not an individual person but figuratively refers to a congregation as a corporate entity (as Jesus addressed churches in Rev. 2–3); "her children," therefore, are individual members of that congregation. John uses this same feminine terminology at the end of this letter ("your chosen sister"—1:13). Those who claim these "ladies" are actual women assume that each of them has multiple Christian children and yet no husbands, fancily weaving these two families and their scenarios into the text.

"[W]hom I love in truth" (1:1b)—as we know from reading his gospel account and his first epistle, "love" and "truth" are John's prominent and special subjects. This is especially the case at a time when serious heresies and doctrinal controversies—i.e., challenges to and malignancies of divine love and divine truth—are confronting him and the early church.

John's love is pure, not shallow, superficial, or with ulterior motive. His love for fellow Christians is defined by Christ's love for His own people (John 13:34–35); it is sincere and wholesome. "[A]nd not only I, but also all who know the truth"—this is the kind of love *all* faithful Christians have toward this "lady" and "her children" (i.e., this congregation). This is also the only kind of love that John says is acceptable among Christians (1 John 5:1–2).

"[F]or the sake of the truth which abides in us and will be with us forever" (1:2) gives the reason behind (or divine support for) this love for fellow believers. Christians have God's truth indwelling us, because we have *believed* in (John 20:31) and *obeyed* it (recall 1 John 2:3–6). The defining foundation of our love does not come from us, either individually or collectively, but from Christ. Just as we have received the Holy Spirit upon baptism into Christ (Acts 2:38, 5:32), so we have received the truth by which He sanctifies us (John 17:17, 1 Peter 1:2). If Christ dwells in us, and the Holy Spirit dwells in us, then divine truth dwells in us.

This indwelling does not (and cannot) mean we are infallible in our understanding of all God has revealed in His word. It does mean, however, that we believe the gospel of Christ to be true, and we have committed ourselves to it. Such are the implications of John's statements about "the truth." "[A]nd will be with us forever" indicates the unfailing, incorruptible, and transcendent nature of divine truth: it is timeless, universal, unchanging, impartial, and factual. As long as we remain faithful to God's truth, it will be with us forever—even beyond the grave.

"Grace, mercy and peace will be with us ..." (1:3a). Paul usually forms this same kind of salutation as a desire or prayer (as in 1 Cor. 1:3); John states it as a fact. Those who "love in truth" are recipients also of God's kindness that leads to salvation. Grace gives to us what we do not deserve; mercy saves us from what we *do* deserve; the result of these gifts is peace with God (Rom. 5:1–2). Everything God the Father does for us comes *through* God the Son.

Walking in Truth (1:4–6): John rejoices over having found "children" of this "lady" walking in truth (1:4).[73] Christians are *commanded* to "walk in truth"; this is not an option. To walk in truth means to live in conformity with the truthful teaching *and* behavior of Jesus Christ

(1 John 2:6). Such conformity also requires the rejection of all those teachings (and fellowship with the people who bring them) that contradict this divinely revealed truth. The Father endears those who are "friends" of Jesus (John 15:10, 14); He loves those who love Jesus (John 16:27).

John asks this "lady"—the congregation to whom he is writing—to "love one another" (1:5–6). "Ask" here indicates a request from one in authority, as well as the concern of one who anticipates danger.[74] Those who imitate Christ must also imitate this love, especially toward others who follow Him (John 13:34–35, 1 John 2:7). Genuine Christian love remains the cure today for all the troubles within the brotherhood.

The ultimate demonstration of genuine love for God *and* His people is through obedience to His commandments (1:6; see John 14:15, 1 John 5:2–3). Those who will not keep His commandments, for any reason, betray their professed love for God. No one can properly love God's people while living in defiance of His commandments. John may have in mind here Gnostics who claim to be Christians, but who reject the fact that Jesus is God's Son. Since such people refuse to walk in truth, then neither do they *love* the truth, God, or His people. The teaching on these things—truth, love, and obedience—is unified and inseparable; these three things rise or fall together.

Those Who Do Not Walk in Truth (1:7–10): Having provided the right teaching on what it means to walk in truth and love, John now turns his attention to those who are walking otherwise. He does not intend to deal with such people through this letter; he did not write to them but to those who are in danger of being infected with their false teaching. It is possible that John will confront these false teachers in person later (as he said he would in 3 John 10 concerning Diotrephes).

"Deceivers" (1:7) are not people who have stumbled into error through an innocent misunderstanding of apostolic teaching. Instead, they are people who *do* know it, but choose to teach something different, and then pawn this different teaching off on others as though it was genuine. Peter describes the same type of people (i.e., "false prophets" and "false teachers") in 2 Peter 2:1–3. These are people who:

- infiltrate the flock of genuine believers to destroy it (Acts 20:29–30). The churches operate on an honor system, which also makes them vulnerable to such infiltration.
- secretly introduce "destructive heresies"—i.e., teachings that are not from God, but are the product of their own self-inflated imagination and incite division amid God's people.
- "[deny] the Master who bought them"—this could be a reference to Gnosticism (in denying the Deity of Jesus, and thus denying the blood He shed to atone for their sins), or it could be a reference to rejecting Jesus' authority (in rejecting His apostles' teaching). In either case, clearly these men are rebels who also seek to win new converts to their twisted gospel.
- use "sensuality" (a word implying filthy lust, unchaste behavior, and shameless excess) as a means of drawing morally weak men and women to their side. Not all "sensuality" is sexual in nature, but it does always indicate a base, carnal appetite for those things associated with the satanic world.

"[M]any deceivers have gone out into the world" (1:7; recall 1 John 2:19, 26, and 4:1–3). "[I]nto the world" indicates a widespread campaign promoted by Satan to obscure God's truth from as many people as possible (2 Cor. 4:3–4). Specifically, these "deceivers" are those who deny that Jesus the Man is also Christ the Son of God—a foundational premise of Gnosticism (see "Introduction to *1 John*").

There is no compatibility between Gnostic teaching and NT theology. Furthermore, the Gnostics offered no *proof* (especially miraculous works—Heb. 2:3–4) that their beliefs were true. Such men claimed to believe in Christ, but not according to apostolic teaching. John defines an "antichrist" as one who claims to be "of Christ" but teaches a purposely misleading doctrine about Him, and therefore makes himself His enemy (Mat. 12:30). See comments on 1 John 2:18 for further exposition.

Since the danger is real, John warns his readers to "watch yourselves" so as not to fall prey to this false teaching (1:8). The NT provides several warnings to believers to *be careful* and not stray from the truth (Mat.

7:15, 10:17, Acts 20:28, 1 Tim. 1:3–4, etc.). Failure to be careful about how you listen (Luke 8:18), who you listen to, what you believe, and how you live will result in losing all that was once gained. Christians must be faithful to the apostolic teaching that led them to Christ in the first place—to endure in sound doctrine (1 Tim. 4:6, 6:3–4a).

John's fear is that Christians will lose "what we have accomplished"— likely, the "we" referring to the apostolic ministry (including his own) among the churches. However, the meaning here may be an editorial "we," meaning, what Christians in general have gained in having received God's good gifts. One's "full reward" simply refers to the "crown of life" he will receive upon his having remained faithful until death (James 1:12, 1 Peter 5:4, and Rev. 2:10). A believer cannot receive anything less than a "full" reward since God does not hand out "half" or "partial" rewards. Either one's reward is complete or lost altogether; there are no other options.

While Paul had been accused by his Jewish opponents of not going far *enough* (i.e., they insisted that he teach Gentile converts to observe also the Law of Moses—see Acts 15:1, 5), John warns of the opposite problem, namely, of going "too far" in one's teaching about Christ (1:9).[75] In this case, a person has creatively *added* to the gospel of Christ his own blends, brands, suppositions, and opinions about "the truth"— then teaches these as though they *are* "the truth." (Sadly, many people today are carried away by this same strategy.)

To go "*too* far" is just as condemnable as not going far *enough*; both misrepresent the truth; both fail to teach the "whole purpose" of God as revealed by Christ's apostles (Acts 20:27). John's response is blunt and explicit: such people "[do] not have God."

It is possible, too, that John is condemning this "too far" teaching in another way as well. The Gnostic teachers claimed to be "advanced thinkers"[76] who possessed special (mystical) knowledge about God, the spiritual realm, etc., beyond what they might have considered "basic Christianity." Thus, John may be saying, "These men claim to be so advanced in their knowledge of God, yet they in fact do not have any fellowship with God." On the other hand, "the one who abides in the [apostolic] teaching, he has both the Father and the Son" (1:9b, bracketed word is mine). John states what believers should avoid (progressing beyond apostolic teaching), then what they should follow (holding fast to sound teaching).

"If anyone comes to you and does not bring this [apostolic] teaching [that Jesus *is* the Son of God], do not receive him into {your} house, and do not give him a greeting …" (1:10, bracketed words are mine).[77] Some Christians have assumed this to mean, "We cannot allow *anyone* into our house who is not a Christian," or " … who belongs to a man-made denomination," or " … who does not believe in the gospel exactly as we do."

Such conclusions ignore the context of this passage. John is not talking about merely what a person privately believes, what church he attends, or whether he professes to be a Christian. John identifies the "anyone" as a person that misrepresents himself as a faithful brother in Christ while teaching a false doctrine *about* Christ. The specific false doctrine John mentions (in this epistle) is one's teaching against the divinity of Jesus, as mentioned earlier.

What John means, then, is that we cannot give personal endorsement to or approval of those who we know to be *false teachers*. We cannot treat these people as fellow Christians, since no one can be a Christian who denies the divinity of Jesus. A common belief about God does not render unimportant all doctrinal differences concerning His Son. And we cannot regard these people as being in good standing with God despite a "disagreement" over Scripture, because their "disagreement" is a modification or corruption of the plain and unmistakable teaching of Scripture. This is not a disagreement over human opinions or private convictions but is rebellion against God's authority.

For this reason, "do not receive him into your house, and do not give him a greeting"—i.e., do not honor him as a fellow Christian; do not regard him (through your invitation) as a sincere believer. He is *not* a brother in Christ; he is *not* sincere. He is an impostor whom Christians need to shun, not someone worthy of welcoming and respect (Rom. 16:17–18). "John is not talking about the traveler who needs lodging for the night. He is referring to the teacher who intends to destroy the church of Jesus Christ."[78]

"Greeting" indicates an expression of joy over seeing someone whom you welcome and respect.[79] Yet Christians should express no joy over someone who is deliberately and maliciously promoting a false gospel about our Lord and Savior. Giving him a joyful welcome makes one an accomplice to that person's wicked deeds (1:11).[80]

Closing Remarks (1:12–13): John's letter is clearly a preface to a much longer discussion, one which he wants to have in person (1:12). "You" in this passage is, in the Greek, plural (as in "all of you"), which again supports the idea that John is writing to an entire congregation and not an individual "lady."[81]

"[F]ace to face" [lit., mouth to mouth] illustrates the personal nature of Christian fellowship. We cannot express genuine brotherly fellowship, affection, compassion, and edification through a letter, e-mail, phone text, emoticon, video conference, or any other impersonal and inadequate means of communication. We are to do these things *face to face*—looking into the other person's eyes, reading their facial expressions and body language, connecting with their physical identity, and reaching out with physical gestures of kindness and affection. For now, John must settle for offering words in a letter; in time, however, he looks forward to meeting with these Christians in the flesh, so to speak.

"The children of your chosen sister greet you" (1:13). Likely, this veiled remark refers to the congregation where John is presently, offering its greetings to the congregation to which John is writing. (Recall remarks on 1:1 and "Introduction to *2 John* and *3 John*.") This common closing salutation suggests that, at a time when enemies of the church (non-believing Jews? Roman officials? Gnostic heretics?) might intercept written communication. If so, a cryptic reference is preferable to an open and literal one.

Questions

1.) Is "walking in truth" (1:4) the same as "walking by faith" (2 Cor. 5:7), "walking by the Spirit" (Gal. 5:16), "walking in the Light" (1 John 1:7), and "walking according to His commandments" (2 John 1:6)?

   a. What does all this "walking" necessarily imply? (There are several answers.)

   b. Why are Christians consistently given a *point of reference* by which to walk—i.e., why are we not to "walk" however or wherever we want, but always *with*, *by*, or *toward* something God has provided?

2.) Why are "deceivers" (1:7) far more dangerous than those who are merely weak, ignorant, and misinformed?

   a. Does this mean that weak, ignorant, and misinformed people—Christians or not—pose no threat to the church? Please explain.

    b. What so often motivates deceivers *to* deceive—i.e., what is in it for them, as they see it? (There are several possible answers.)

3.) Does John's warning (in 1:9–11) forbid bringing your denominationalist, Jewish, Muslim, Buddhist, agnostic, atheistic, or irreligious friends and family members into your home under *any* circumstance?

    a. If so, is this consistent with the *context* of this epistle, or is this something that some Christians may have read *into* it? What is the difference between these two things?

    b. If not, might there be circumstances in which John *does* mean that you are *not* to welcome these people into your home?

Lesson Eleven
The Third Epistle of John
(3 John)

Salutation (1:1–2): Whereas John wrote to an unnamed "chosen lady" in his second epistle (likely, a veiled reference to a congregation's elders rather than an individual person), his third epistle is addressed to Gaius, a specific Christian man. Gaius is "beloved" of John (used twice in the salutation), at least as a faithful brother in Christ and likely a dear friend.

"[W]hom I love in truth"—i.e., to whom John expresses honest and unspoiled brotherly love. No love is worth anything that is not "in truth"; and no truth can accomplish anything good that is not in love. "I pray …" (1:2)—John expresses genuine concern not only for Gaius' spiritual well-being, but also his physical health and personal prosperity. He has been praying for all of these on Gaius' behalf.

Walking in the Truth (1:3–4): Maintaining the theme of his first two epistles, John speaks of "walking in truth" (1:3). Apparently, some traveling Christians, possibly having been initially sent out by John himself, have brought back a very good report about Gaius and the kindness he showed them (to be discussed in 1:5–8). These men "testified" or gave an eyewitness account of Gaius' honest and upright behavior ("your truth"), and how he is "walking in truth" (God's truth). Thus, Gaius' "truth" is consistent with God's truth, and so proves Gaius' righteous attitude and conduct. This, understandably, brings John great joy (1:4).

"I have no greater joy than this, to hear of my children walking in the truth" (1:4; see 1 John 1:4). When Christ's people live in conformity with Him—for no other reason than their love for Him and their desire to please Him—this brings Him great joy. When Christ's joy is in His believers, then they also are filled with joy (John 15:11, 17:13). "My children" is John's tender reference to Christians (recall 1 John 2:1), a term Paul also used in the same way (Gal. 4:19). The difference between "your children" in 2 John 1:4 and "my children" in the present verse may be explained as follows: "His [John's] children" are those whom he converted, taught, and/or groomed for their own ministries (such as Gaius); "your children" are Christians with whom John did not have such direct involvement.[82]

Accepting "Strangers" (1:5–8): In this next section, John commends Gaius for his kindness toward Christians who were "strangers" to him but whom he treated as *friends*. "Strangers" [Greek, *xenos*] does not here carry the same meaning that the word suggests in modern language. Today, a stranger is someone with no connection to us, whom we tend to avoid, and whom we may perceive as dangerous ("A stranger walked into the room with me when I was alone, and I bristled with apprehension"). But in the ancient world, people regarded strangers differently, as simply someone unknown, and thus having no previous history or interaction. It can also be a person of a different ancestry, culture, or community.

In the present case (1:5), "strangers" has a specific reference: Christians who were simply unknown to Gaius at the time when he showed them hospitality. We know this because John uses the word in this very context; he defines them interchangeably with "brethren"; and Gaius gave them this treatment with this understanding. These are not just drifters seeking refuge wherever they could find it and end up on Gaius' doorstep; they are not lazy people who rely only upon the kindness of others while they themselves remain irresponsible (as described in 2 Thess. 3:6–10). Rather, these are men who "went out for the sake of the Name (1:7)—i.e., they are on church business, so to speak, and are likely traveling Christians who are sharing the gospel of Christ with those who have not yet heard it.

John commends Gaius for having treated these men well and encourages him to *continue* to do so. Outside of our own families, we are to take care of Christians "especially." We are all *born* as God's children, in the most basic understanding, since He is the Father of all humankind. Christians alone are *made* God's children, having been "born" of Him (John 1:12–13, 1 John 3:1–2), and therefore are brought into a spiritual family, the "household of God" (1 Tim. 3:15). Thus, while Christians are to show godly love to all people, even to our own enemies (Mat. 5:43–47), we are to show a *special demonstration* of that love to those who belong to Christ.

Gaius did not just *think* about showing kindness to these traveling Christians; he *in fact* showed them such kindness. "No greater compliment could be paid to Gaius than that John should take for granted that Gaius will do what is not even asked but is only implied."[83] These Christians did not return to John saying, "Gaius *meant* to show us kindness, but we never received it"; rather, he meant it and showed it—and they actually received it. They not only gave John himself a good report, but they "testified to your love before the church" (1:6)—i.e., to the entire congregation.

"You would do well to send them [i.e., future Christian travelers—MY WORDS] on their way in a manner worthy of God." A "manner worthy" indicates a known expectation that alone is right and fitting; it also implies that anything different than this would be unworthy. God's word provides the written instruction for all worthy behavior; Jesus Christ provides the model example of it (John 5:19, 13:13–15, etc.). Thus, John is not leaving it up to Gaius to decide arbitrarily when, how, or to whom he is to show Christian kindness; instead, he is alluding to a known and authoritative standard of behavior which he expects Gaius to follow.

These traveling Christians—once "strangers" to Gaius, but no longer—"went out for the sake of the Name" (1:7).[84] "Name" here refers to the venerated Name of God or Jesus Christ. The *Name* of deity is something to be honored and defended, just as the *word* of deity is to be honored (1 Tim. 6:1 and Titus 2:5). Failure to honor the Name of God—whether in speech, personal behavior, or one's conduct toward others—is offensive to Him, just as the Law teaches (Exod. 20:7, Lev. 10:3).

John's message to Gaius is that, since these traveling Christians went out for the *sake* of "the Name," they deserve respectful treatment from those who are *also* of "the Name." Fellow believers are to support the honorable nature of their mission—an indication for us today that, even though we may not personally be on a "mission" to spread the gospel, we are to support those who *are*.

Furthermore, these travelers "accepted nothing from the Gentiles" (1:7b)—lit., the heathens, pagans, or foreigners (to the Christian religion). Originally, a "Gentile" meant anyone who was not a Jew (as in Mat. 10:5); since the advent of the church, however, Christians have used the term in non-biblical writings to mean those who are not Christians. The travelers of whom John speaks relied only on the hospitality of fellow believers, not the help of unbelievers.

There are at least two reasons for this:

- **First,** believers in Christ should support fellow believers, just as they should compensate those who preach the gospel to them (1 Cor. 9:14). Similarly, when Jesus sent out His disciples to the cities of Israel, He expected those who looked forward to the coming kingdom of God to support those who proclaimed it (Mat. 10:40–41). "Had they [i.e., strangers] accepted hospitality from 'the Gentiles,' it might have given the impression that their own people did not support them adequately."[85]
- **Second,** Christians should rely upon God's care for them as demonstrated *through* the kindness of fellow believers, rather than trust in their own resources or provisions (2 Cor. 9:8–11).

The work of evangelists is to preach and teach the gospel; the work of other Christians is to support these men however they can (1 Cor. 16:15–16). This is John's point in 1:8: "we ought to support such men"—i.e., not just *you* (Gaius), but *all* Christians. In doing so, we participate in (or, become partakers of) "the truth" proclaimed by them. Paul has said that we become "fellow partaker[s]" of the gospel when we exercise our Christian liberties for the gospel's sake (1 Cor. 9:23). Similarly, whether you are the preacher, the one financially supporting the preacher, or the one setting up the chairs and microphones for those who come to hear the preacher's message, *you all* (Paul and John both say) are "fellow workers with [or, for] the truth."

Contrast of Two Men (1:9–12): We do not know what the "something" is that John wrote to the church (1:9a), but it may have been either (what we call) *1 John* or *2 John*. It is possible, too, that this "something"

John wrote has been lost to history.⁸⁶ Regardless, whatever John wrote with his apostolic authority ought to be listened to and not resisted or rejected. Apostles are Christ's hand-picked ambassadors (Mat. 10:1–4) who have received authority to speak on His behalf (Heb. 2:3–4, 2 Peter 3:1–2). Their commands carry the weight of the Holy Spirit who has inspired them to speak (1 Cor. 14:37). Furthermore, John has already said in his first epistle that he who listens to Christ's apostles "knows God," while he who does not "is not from God" (1 John 4:6). This still holds true today.

Which church John wrote to—the church where Gaius attends, another church, or *the* church—we do not know, but we do know Diotrephes disregarded it.⁸⁷ What position Diotrephes holds in "the church" to which John wrote is not known; possibly he is an elder, or even a preacher. In any case, in rejecting John's apostolic authority, he makes his *own* authority superior to it. Notice John says, "I wrote … ," then that Diotrephes does not accept "what we say" [or, simply, "us"], going from singular to plural. John implies *all* the apostles when he writes with the *authority* of an apostle; to receive or reject one is to receive or reject them all.

Diotrephes' *reason* for rejecting John's written instructions is his own pride: he "loves to be first among [the members of the congregation—MY WORDS]." When Jesus' disciples argued over which of them should be first among them ("the greatest"), the Master responded: "[T]he one who is the greatest among you must become like the youngest, and the leader like the servant" (Luke 22:26). Diotrephes failed to learn this basic lesson in humility and servitude; just as he did not listen to Jesus' teachings, so he dismissed John's as well. Jesus also said, "Whoever exalts himself shall be humbled; and whoever humbles himself shall be exalted (Mat. 12:12)"—another lesson lost on proud and arrogant Diotrephes.

"For this reason"—i.e., because he will not listen to what I *write*—"if I come, I will call attention to his deeds"—i.e., I will shame him to his face (1:10). It seems whenever men speak God's word to any given congregation, there will always be someone (or a group of people) who thinks he is above all that, above the law, exempt from its instruction, smarter than the apostles, and even smarter than God.[88] Such arrogance has plagued the church from the beginning, and sadly it will always be a thorn in the church's side. Yet, these same people cannot contend with the power (to perform miracles) or the authority (to condemn before God) that the apostles possess, just as Paul warned the Corinthians (1 Cor. 4:18–21).

John is not certain when or if he will come to confront Diotrephes, but he makes it clear that he *will* confront him if given the opportunity. John has no reason to fear this man, or any man who challenges him; he knows he is right, wields heavenly authority, and can denounce or punish as needed. There is another reason for this: Diotrephes is not just rejecting John's message to the church; he is also "accusing us with wicked words" (1:10). This phrase is unique to the NT, and refers to someone who is speaking nonsense, malicious or empty charges, or idle rants.[89]

In the present case, however, it is "not simply foolish chatter, but malevolent words."[90] We get the idea that Diotrephes, *upon* rejecting John's words, takes opportunity to personally berate and ridicule John as well ("Who does this man think he is?"; "I am fully capable of handling my own congregation—I do not need the counsel of this know-it-all"; "I am not about to lower myself to John's self-serving instructions"; etc.).

As if this were not enough, John says, "he himself does not receive the brethren, either" (1:10)—i.e., these are the brethren whom Gaius *did* receive, whom John may have sent out. Not only does Diotrephes reject John's writing, but he also rejects those who carry the letter sent by him. Diotrephes is "not satisfied" with only dismissing John's instruction; he also dismisses his courtesy toward and rightful acknowledgement of those who are Christ's "brethren." As if *this* were not enough, he also imposes his self-determined authority upon the members of his congregation (which includes Gaius?) who *do* show decency and brotherly kindness toward those whom Diotrephes rejects.

"[A]nd puts {them} out of the church"—"them" is supplied by the translators because it is implied in the text. This may refer to the traveling

Christians, especially those who abide by John's teachings and were sent by him, and/or those members of the congregation who sided with these other men rather than with Diotrephes. It is always amazing how much trouble one man can cause for Christians who are simply trying to do what is right.

"Beloved"—the fourth time in this short epistle John has referred to Gaius in this way—"do not imitate what is evil, but what is good" (1:11a). He is not admonishing Gaius in the least, since Gaius has already demonstrated good works. Yet, John wants to reinforce those good decisions Gaius has made and encourage him not to succumb to Diotrephes' unchristian behavior, whether because of that man's strong influence, peer pressure from those of a similar mind, or weariness of doing good because of the difficulties involved (Gal. 6:9–10).

"The one who does good is of God; the one who does evil has not seen God" (1:11b). This is a brief form of what John said in his first epistle (1 John 2:29, 3:10, 4:7–8, etc.). One who is genuinely "of God" cannot practice sinful behavior any more than one who is "evil" can claim fellowship with Him (1 John 1:5–6, 2:4). John supports what Jesus said about one's inward character being manifested by outward behavior (Mat. 7:17–18). Diotrephes is a bad tree (i.e., has a bad heart) because of the bad "fruit" he has produced over time, even against direct instruction to do otherwise.

In sharp contrast, John points to another man, Demetrius, who "has received a good testimony from everyone, and from the truth itself" (1:12a). We know nothing of this man other than what John wrote here; yet, what he *did* write reveals his honorable character. Everyone who knows Demetrius speaks well of him; he has an excellent reputation within the brotherhood. Not only do men speak well of him, but so does "the truth itself"—i.e., the divine standard of righteousness which determines how close or far away people are (so to speak) from God.

Demetrius is the exact opposite of Diotrephes; so is Gaius, but it may be that Demetrius has an even greater reputation and/or a longer history of doing good than Gaius does. "[A]nd we add our testimony …"

(1:12b)—i.e., John gives his personal endorsement to Demetrius, which is worth more (in value and authority) than the testimonies of others, simply because of his position as an apostle of Christ. "Our" refers to members of the church John attends, or those who work closely with him in the work of the church of Christ.

Closing Remarks and Farewell (1:13–15): "I had many things to write to you, but …" (1:13–14)—this is almost verbatim of what John had written to the noble "lady" in 2 John 1:12. When it comes to giving apostolic direction, John is willing to write whatever needs to be said; yet, when it comes to personal friendship, Christian fellowship, and the joy these bring, he wants that to be done "face to face" [lit., mouth to mouth, an idiom for a conversational exchange among friends].

"Peace be to you" (1:15)—a cordial and well-intended expression that wishes general goodness and prosperity upon another person (recall 1:2). In the case of Christian fellowship, however, this means far more than it does among unbelievers (John 14:27). No one can *truly* be at peace with God who is not in fellowship with Him; and those who are in fellowship with God are to dwell upon this peace through prayer and thanksgiving (Phil. 4:6–7). It would be altogether improper for John to say to Diotrephes, for example, "Peace be to you," since he stands contrary to God and therefore *cannot* be at peace with Him (compare Acts 8:21–23).

"The friends" refers to fellow Christians, since we are all "friends" with and through Christ (John 15:14). In other cases, "friends" are those who have a closer relationship to another Christian than all other Christians would have (as in Acts 24:23). "Greet the friends by name"—John is no doubt thinking of specific people in Gaius' congregation to whom he wishes to impart his personal greeting, but allows Gaius to do this on his behalf, rather than John simply mentioning their names in a letter.

Questions

1.) John's words to Gaius teach that Christians are to show hospitality to fellow Christians who are "strangers" to us (1:5). What does he mean by "strangers" in this context?

   a. Is there any responsibility on the part of the "strangers" to prove their authenticity to *us*—or should we just trust them at their word and ask no questions?

   b. Sometimes people say (in the absence of doing anything), "It's the thought that counts." How would John respond to this sentiment regarding Christians taking care of other Christians? Are "thoughts" of hospitality equal to acts of hospitality?

2.) John describes Diotrephes as one who "loves to be first among" the brethren (1:9). What does he mean by this? How might this personality manifest itself in a congregation today?

   a. Do *we* (Christians) have the right to put out of *our* congregations those whom we believe are a threat to our group? If so, how is this different from what Diotrephes did? If not, why not?

b. Do we (Christians) have the right or ability to put people out of Jesus' church? Why or why not?

3.) Demetrius, unlike Diotrephes, is praised by John as having a "good testimony ... from the truth itself" (1:12). What does John mean by this?

a. When someone says today, "I'm a good person," is it their opinion, the opinion of others, or God's truth that substantiates this? Why is the *source* of one's goodness of critical importance, especially considering our future presentation before God?

b. Will "the truth" testify favorably about *you*? (No need to reveal your answer to others, but this is something you ought to ask yourself.)

Introduction to *Jude*

The *Epistle of Jude* is, sadly, one of the least studied books of the NT. This, because it is brief (and therefore deemed unworthy of attention), and because some have disputed its authenticity (see below). Adding to its unpopularity is its unusual style and seeming irrelevant content. To many, it may seem more "bewildering" than profitable.[91] Yet, the more one studies and understands Jude's epistle, the more one realizes just how *eye-opening* and *relevant* it is for what churches face today.

There is no question that Jude's writing style is markedly different from that of Paul or John. His writing is poetic, forceful, and often dark. It is as though he cannot unleash his denunciations of false teachers fast enough, but breathlessly rushes to the next round immediately after he finishes the first. "Its style is broken and rugged, bold and picturesque, energetic, vehement, glowing with the fires of passion."[92] For this reason, it is hard to read *Jude* without stopping: one thought spills into the next in a cascade of thoughts that continue from verse 3 to the end of the epistle.

Jude's subject matter immediately seizes the reader's attention. He speaks of insidious men creeping into the church like a spiritual darkness or an unholy presence. He then talks about God's judgment against unbelievers, fallen angels, and Sodom and Gomorrah. From there, he goes into a prolonged denunciation of false teachers, highlighting their spiritual bankruptcy with colorful and graphic imagery. After this, he turns his attention to faithful Christians and what they must do to contend earnestly against such spiritually deviant men. He ends his epistle with one of the longest and most eloquent doxologies (i.e., hymns of praise to God) in the NT. Word for word and subject for subject, there is more compacted into this single-chapter epistle than might be found across several chapters of much longer NT books.

Purpose for Writing: Jude's references to the OT (and non-biblical Jewish sources) indicate that his target audience, while not specifically stated, may be Jewish Christians.[93] Yet, it is impossible to know this for certain. It could also be that Jude quotes from what he knows best—the Hebrew Bible (our Old Testament). There is not enough internal evidence—and virtually no external evidence—for us to know for certain who the original recipients of this letter were, but we are certain Jude *himself* knew this. In the most general sense, he is writing to all Christians in churches that are directly facing the problems he addresses in his letter.

One thing we do know: Jude intended to write about the "common salvation" enjoyed by Christians everywhere—no doubt a positive and edifying letter—but he felt compelled to urge his readers to "contend earnestly for the faith" (1:3). The reason for this urgent appeal is because of a new and dangerous threat against the churches in the first century. This danger, in the form of erroneous teaching as well as those who propagated it, had infiltrated various churches, and maligned the gospel of Christ. Jude felt "the necessity" to address this in writing—a motivation no doubt prompted by the Holy Spirit. Barclay says, "It may be that Jude never again got the chance to write the treatise he had planned; but the fact is that he did more for the church by writing this urgent little letter than he could possibly have done by leaving a long treatise on faith."[94] Woods adds, "The Epistle of Jude was written to meet the need of the hour in which it was produced, and this circumstance determined its form and content."[95]

The people in error whom Jude describes may well be Gnostic teachers, although his description is less direct than John's (in *1 John*). Yet, if Jude's epistle was written before the fall of Jerusalem (AD 70), this would pre-date the threat of Gnosticism in the churches by several decades, making this unlikely. A better conclusion is that Jude spoke out against what is known as "antinomianism"—the teaching that, once in Christ, one no longer needs to follow God's laws [*anti-* = against, *nomos* = law]. More simply, it is like the modern "once saved, always saved" mentality: there is nothing one can do to fall from grace once he has it, so there is no need to keep commandments *or* refrain from sinful behavior. This allows for a sensual, hedonistic, and careless version of Christianity that, as Jude says, "[turns] the grace of our God into licentiousness [i.e., recklessness or depravity]" (1:4, bracketed words added).

The contemporary relevance of Jude's epistle is startling. Today, Christ's churches are assaulted with much of the same kind of problem Jude *describes*; likewise, the Christians' response to these problems are the same as Jude *prescribes*.

- **First,** we need to "contend earnestly for the faith": we must know what this means, how to do it, and be *actively doing* it. We have people today posing as Christians (or, who are Christians but have accepted very unchristian teachings) who downplay the need for active love of the brethren, service to God, holy living, and sound teaching. Instead, they wish to absolve themselves of responsibility to the church, live however they want, embrace ungodly lifestyles, and abandon the NT pattern.
- **Second,** faithful Christians must recognize—just as Jude emphatically declares—that God is very much aware of these people and the emptiness of their teaching. Just as He brought justice against people (and angels) in ages past, so He will to all those who are presently trading their loyalty to Christ for a gratuitous indulgence in a self-defined but pathetic version of "Christianity."
- **Third,** faithful Christians must do exactly what Jude *said* to resist such people and their teaching: remember the words of Christ and His apostles; build themselves up in holy faith; pray in the Spirit; keep themselves in the love of God; etc. (1:17–23). To "contend earnestly" does not mean sit in pews on Sundays and listen to well-scripted sermons; it does not mean sit back and let others (elders, deacons, preachers, etc.) do the dirty work of the church; and it does not mean remain unequipped and unprepared to confront any error that seeks to destroy the churches. Rather, it means *all* faithful Christians must be involved in resisting and confronting error that threatens churches or the brotherhood.

Questions of Canonicity: "Canonicity" (in reference to the Bible) refers formally and rightfully recognizing written works as belonging to the body of inspired literature we call "Scripture." Some books or letters were immediately canonized (such as many of Paul's writings); others, such as *Jude*, were slow to be universally accepted into the body of the NT. Its brevity, unusual content, and lack of apostolic claims made the decision to accept *Jude* as canonical—i.e., a book worthy of being included in our NT—challenging. While it was used frequently in the churches themselves, it still met resistance from the emerging class of scholarly historians overseeing NT literature in the early centuries after Christ.

> The men of the Reformation [16th century] voiced doubts as to its canonical standing, and since then various commentators have for various reasons shared these doubts. The critics claim that Jude is a forgery like Second Peter. Why a second-century writer [i.e., the alleged forger] should select such a minor man as Jude to forge an epistle in his name is difficult to understand. Why one forger should utilize another forger [i.e., referring to the similarities between *Jude* and *2 Peter*] is still more incredible …[96]

There is no question that *Jude* and *2 Peter* are remarkably close in design. For this reason, some have chosen *2 Peter* over *Jude*, assuming that if Jude copied Peter's letter, it lacks genuineness; others have dismissed them both as being equally lacking in genuineness.[97] Apart from divine inspiration, the odds that both men wrote virtually the same letter independent of each other are extremely slim.

On the other hand, there is no reason to *doubt* divine inspiration of either or both letters just because one borrowed from the other. Matthew and Luke, it appears, both copied material from Mark to a degree, yet all Christians regard both are as inspired writings. Copying, by itself, is not the problem; the problem (if it is even a problem at all) is, who copied whom? Did Peter copy Jude, or did Jude copy Peter? Peter wrote to Gentiles; Jude, to Jews (or so it appears). Both men could use the same well-known material to reach different audiences in different ways.

In the end, it really does not matter who copied or did not copy: both letters have been accepted into the NT canon (the authoritative and inspired literature of Christ's church), having met the criteria necessary for this. The Third Council of Carthage (AD 397) formally recognized *Jude* in the NT canon,[98] but the evidence for its inclusion far pre-dates this. Since the earliest church "fathers" (Clement of Alexandria, Origen, Tertullian, et al), *Jude* has been regarded as an authentic and inspired epistle.[99] In the Modern Era, there has been little serious challenge to the genuineness of this epistle or its inclusion in the NT.

Author and Date of Writing: The fact that Jude does not reveal himself as an apostle, but instead as merely "a bond-servant of Jesus Christ" and "brother of James" indicates he is *not* Jude the apostle (Luke 6:16). In fact, he humbly exalts his brother James over himself, even though he has as much right to be honored as Jesus' physical brother as what James enjoyed (Gal. 1:19). "The title which he assumes, 'brother of James,' was evidently chosen because the James referred to was well-known, and because the fact that he was his brother would be a sufficient designation of himself, and of his right to address Christians in this manner."[100]

Some have suggested that *Jude* was written pseudonymously—i.e., it is the work of some unknown ("pseudo") author who attaches a *known* author's name to it to give it credibility and gain readership. But since Jude is a common name in the first century, and the writer did not make himself *specifically* known to us, this theory does not hold weight. The claim of authorship by someone who is *not* the author immediately calls into question the content of those writings.

As to the date of writing of the *Epistle of Jude*, no one knows for certain. A good guess is a pre-destruction of Jerusalem date (i.e., before AD 70), but we cannot prove this. The content provides almost no dative evidence. An early date (say, prior to AD 50) seems very unlikely, since the problems Jude addresses are what second or even third generation churches encounter, not newly established churches filled with first-generation believers.

Cogdill's quote sums up the consensus of most conservative commentators: "The general date of the letter written by Jude is indicated by the fact that it deals with the same problems, teaches the same truths, and makes to some degree the same arguments against those problems that are made in Second Peter. The indication, therefore, is that it was written around the same time as Second Peter and can be dated somewhere around 66 to 67 AD."[101]

Salutation
(Jude 1:1–2)

"Jude" [or, Judas] (1:1a) has traditionally been identified as the physical brother of James, both men being physical brothers of Jesus, all biological sons of Mary (Mat. 13:55, Mark 6:3). This is a far more logical conclusion than assuming him to be Christ's apostle by the same name (Luke 6:16, John 14:22, and Acts 1:13).[102] (See "Introduction: Author and Date of Writing" for more details.)

The term "bond-servant" often meant a house slave, one who has surrendered himself to live in his master's house to serve him and his family; in the most general sense, one bound to a master.[103] In the ancient world, men could become voluntary or involuntary slaves, depending upon their circumstances; in the present case, Jude's servitude is obviously voluntary. The fact that Jude is a physical brother of Jesus who also describes himself as a servant (slave) of Jesus presents no problem here. All people are slaves of someone or something; all Christians are "slaves of Christ" (Eph. 6:6) and "slaves of righteousness" (Rom. 6:18).

"To those who are the called" (1:1b) refers to believers called by the Holy Spirit through the gospel of Christ (2 Thess. 2:13–14) who have responded in obedience, themselves having called upon the name of the Lord for salvation (Acts 2:21, 22:16, and Rom. 10:13). The "called" are those who belong to Christ—Christians by name—having been called out of the world and into His body of believers, His church (Rom. 1:6). Jude's intention, then, is to write a general letter to all Christians, not to a specific group of Christians in a certain city or region. Specifically, however, he writes to those—whoever they are—being assaulted by false teachers whom he will identify shortly.

"[B]eloved in the God the Father"—lit., those loved by God.[104] The Father loves those who love His Son (John 16:27). Though God loves *all* people (John 3:16), He has a special love (or, a special expression of love) toward those who are in fellowship with Him: the relationship factor changes everything. "[K]ept for Jesus Christ" carries the idea of divine protection or preservation of those whom God loves. Christians enjoy a measure of divine oversight that guards them from falling *if* they do what God says—i.e., put on the full armor of God (Eph. 6:10–17), take the "way of escape" from temptation (1 Cor. 10:13), be diligent to "add" to their faith (2 Peter 1:5–7), etc.

Jude's point, then, is that Christians most certainly do have a special place in God's heart: we are specially loved by Him *because* of His Son, and we are specially preserved by Him *for* His Son. "May mercy and peace and love be multiplied to you" (1:2) recalls Aaron the high priest's benediction on behalf of Israel (Num. 6:22–27):

> Then the LORD [Jehovah] spoke to Moses, saying, "Speak to Aaron and to his sons, saying, 'Thus you shall bless the sons of Israel. You shall say to them:
>   The LORD bless you, and keep you;
>   The LORD make His face shine on you, and be gracious to you;
>   The LORD lift up His countenance on you, and give you peace.'
> So they shall invoke My name on the sons of Israel, and I then will bless them."

Jude's request is not a mere poetic expression any more than Aaron's benediction was. It is a prayerful request for the church as well as an exhortation for Christians to remember the privileged place they have as God's called and chosen people.

Lesson Twelve
Condemnation of Ungodly Men (Jude 1:3–16)

Jude's Reason for Writing (1:3–4): When he first intended to write to the church, Jude had a different kind of epistle in mind than what he ended up with. Originally, he wanted "to write to you about our common salvation"—something he made "every effort" to do (1:3). This says something about Jude's role in the early church, namely, that he is someone both *expected* and *qualified* to write such things to the brethren.

The word "common" means shared, joint, or mutual rather than ordinary in form, regular in time, or unholy or unclean in status (as in Acts 10:14).[105] The message or gospel of salvation is a shared one; it is common to all who call upon the name of the Lord. We are all saved by the same message, for the same reason, by the same method, and by the same Savior. It is also something God *delivered* to us—we did not produce it; we did not empower it with our own human authority.

Thus, the message of truth has already been revealed and delivered. Its content is permanent; it will never be superseded, amended, or modified. Accordingly, Paul preached the same thing in every church (1 Cor. 4:17) and placed a divine curse upon those who would modify or pervert the one gospel he preached (Gal. 1:6–8). "Salvation" is, of course, a relative term: we are "saved" by God through Christ, but the full realization of this salvation—i.e., our entrance into heaven—is conditioned upon our faithful endurance in the things to which we committed ourselves upon our conversion to Christ.

The phrase "contend earnestly" (1:3b) comes from a single Greek word that indicates an intense struggle.[106] "The word 'contend' was used to describe athletic exertion and competitive energy … and it often meant 'wrestling.' Jude calls upon his readers to fight for the faith."[107] One of the most common factors of declining or dying churches today is Christians being content to hear *sermons* on "the faith" but unwilling to *contend* for it. The gospel is worthy of our defense of it, and no one can be better prepared to defend it than noble-minded Christians. To "contend earnestly" does not mean to be *contentious* or *rude*, but to make strenuous effort to teach the faith, defend it, and promote it.

"[T]he faith which was once handed down to all the saints" (1:3b) is specific, in the context of the NT. It refers not to any one individual's faith (as in, a personal faith), but a divinely revealed and objectively defined belief system that *all* Christians believe in, are saved by, and practice (the "one faith" of Eph. 4:5). It encompasses all the teachings of the gospel message concerning Christ and His plan of redemption. This "faith" was "handed down" or delivered to "the saints"—i.e., to Christians—by Christ Himself, as revealed by the Holy Spirit, then taught by His apostles (Eph. 3:1–7, Heb. 2:3–4, and 2 Peter 3:1–2).

Jude now reveals why he has preempted his original message with an admonition to "contend earnestly for the faith": "[C]ertain persons have crept in unnoticed …" (1:4). (He will describe these "certain persons" shortly.) These have surreptitiously slipped into the churches, feigning genuine faith and brotherly love, but with an ulterior motive and a wicked agenda (Mat. 7:15–20, Acts 20:29–30, and Gal. 2:4). The manner in which they have infiltrated the churches—creeping in sneakily rather than being honest and transparent—identifies them as enemies rather than allies.[108]

Such men have been "long beforehand marked out for this condemnation"—i.e., this *type* of people (impostors, wolves, predators, etc.) have been described and identified in writing long before these "certain persons" ever appeared. This no doubt refers to the OT writings that condemned false witnesses, false teachers, and false prophets (Deut. 5:20, Jer. 5:26–31, 14:14, Ezek. 22:28, etc.).

Such "ungodly [or, godless]" men "turn the grace of our God into licentiousness [or, unbridled sensuality]"—a reference to those who claim that divine grace makes *allowance* or even gives *permission* for wanton behavior (since God allegedly will freely and automatically forgive such people). This is consistent with Gnostic teachings that erroneously separate one's spiritual fellowship with God from his earthly conduct, as though the one (spiritual life) has no bearing upon the other (earthly life).

Simply put, such men teach that a person could live a promiscuous, immoral, and unholy life *and still* identify as a righteous Christian (like people do today). Such false teaching denies the holy and righteous lifestyle exemplified in "our only Master and Lord, Jesus Christ": it misrepresents His gospel *and* profanes His holy and righteous life.

"Certain Men" Identified and Condemned (1:5–16): In a passage similar to 2 Peter 2:4–9, Jude comforts his readers with the fact that, despite these "certain men" having infiltrated the brotherhood of saints, they will be held accountable and destroyed by God.[109] This has happened before, he says, and cites three examples:

- ❑ God saved Israel ("a people") from Egypt, but not all *remained* saved (or, preserved by His providence). Those Israelites who "did not believe" in the Lord (1:5) were subsequently condemned to die in the wilderness, being under a divine curse (Num. 14:26–37, Heb. 3:16–19). Not only this, but God destroyed others for their unbelief in separate accounts (see 1 Cor. 10:5–10). In other words, while impostors and unbelievers may creep in undetected among His people, God knows who they are and is fully capable of exercising divine judgment against them.
- ❑ Not only are men held accountable for their rebellion against God, but so are "angels who did not keep their own domain, but abandoned their proper abode" (1:6), whom we call "fallen angels" because of such abandonment.[110] Jude's point is: if God will punish disobedient angels—beings greater in nature and power than men—then certainly He will punish disobedient men.[111] The "great day" is no doubt the Final Judgment (Rev. 20:11–15), the occasion when God will formally sentence these wicked angels for their crimes (Mat. 8:29).[112]
- ❑ As a final example of God's ability to execute judgment against ungodly men, Jude cites His divine judgment against Sodom, Gomorrah, and nearby cities (1:7; see Gen. 19). These cities

"indulged in gross immorality" [lit., gave themselves over to sexual fornication]. The extent to which they were steeped in immorality is then cited: they "went after strange flesh"—i.e., men exercised degrading passion toward other men, and had sexual relations with them, which is homosexuality (Rom. 1:26–28).[113] Nonetheless, Jude's point is not only to condemn homosexuality, but to show that ungodly men who do not repent of their sin—homosexuality or otherwise—are not going to escape divine wrath, and neither will those who creep into His churches to sow false teachings and "doctrines of demons" (1 Tim. 4:1). What happened to these cities, consumed by fire from the Lord (Gen. 19:24), serves as an example of the *eternal* fire that will consume wicked men.

"Yet …" (1:8)—i.e., despite the historical examples of divine wrath, punishment of wicked men and angels, and all the warnings of Scripture, these "certain men" boldly and arrogantly go where angels fear to tread (compare 2 Peter 2:10ff). "Dreaming" indicates living in a false reality, letting one's imagination become the standard of behavior rather than the fixed, absolute, and moral standard of God's word.[114] They "defile the flesh" with sexual immorality (recall 1:4), reject Jesus' authority and the authority of His apostles, and "revile angelic majesties" [lit., speak evil of (heavenly) dignities]. This latter phrase refers to these men assuming an authority (to speak, act, or promote as church doctrine) that not even angels will claim, as evident in the following verse.

Jude cites "Michael the archangel" (1:9) as though we already know him, and indeed he has been mentioned in Dan. 10:13, 21, and 12:1, where he is referred to as "one of the chief princes" of heaven who fights on behalf of God's people. "Archangel" means a chief or captain of angels, implying a hierarchy among angels otherwise unknown to us. Jude's point here is merely to underscore what has just been said: Michael would not assume divine authority in disputing with "the devil" (Satan) over the disposition of Moses' body (Deut. 34:5–6), but these false teachers who have crept into the churches have no such respect, restraint, or humility.

"But"—because of their arrogance, spiritual ignorance, and lack of reverence for God's holiness—"these [certain] men revile the things which they do not understand" (1:10, bracketed word added). Michael understood, Jude understood, and any genuine Christian understands, but these men remain blinded by their own self-inflated egos. They speak evil of what is holy and sanction what is evil. They do not act with reason, intelligence, and discretion, but with animal-like instinct, gratifying whatever lust or sexual desire that comes to mind (1 Thess. 4:3–5, 2 Peter 2:12).

Jude then interjects a "Woe to them!" (1:11). A "woe" (in this context) is a condemnation by or curse from God (as in Luke 6:24–26). Then Jude cites three other instances in which men have received such "woes":

- **Cain**, the first natural son of Creation, and the first son of Adam and Eve, also bears the shame of being the first murderer in all human history (Gen. 4:1–12). The "way of Cain" is the path that defies God, allows sin to master one's heart, and shows no respect for human life (or other people in general). This is exactly what these "certain men" are doing who have crept into the churches: while not having actually murdered, they are categorized *with* murderers because of their failure to *love* the brethren.
- **Balaam**, the prophet-for-hire ("diviner") who—likely, for payment (2 Peter 2:15–16)—incited the Moabite and Midianite women to seduce the Israelites with idolatry and sexual fornication (Num. 25, 31:16). This account is also parallel with what these "certain men" are doing: inciting Christians to engage in sexual fornication and other fleshly indulgences, thus corrupting and incapacitating these people in the same way the Midianite women did the Israelite men.
- **Korah**, the Levite who assumed he could override God's appointment of Moses and Aaron—or simply ignore them—and exalted himself against these men in front of the entire congregation of Israel (Num. 16). God responded by executing Korah and his 250 co-conspirators. In like manner, the "certain men" whom Jude describes have arose within God's churches and disparaged Christ's own authority and His decision to appoint certain men (apostles).

So then, Jude identifies three kinds of people: those whose hearts are given over to sin; those who incite God's people to sin; and those who, blinded by arrogance, do not hesitate to exalt themselves against divine authority. Such men have *gone* in the wrong direction (the "way of Cain"); they have *"rushed headlong"* into error rather than merely being mistaken in their understanding; and they will *perish* because of this—i.e., they will lose their souls (just as Korah and others lost their lives) in divine judgment against them.

To further illustrate the vanity, emptiness, and hopelessness of such men, Jude follows with a poetic description of them (1:12–13), citing examples taken from nature.

- **"These are the men who are hidden reefs in your love feasts when they feast with you without fear, caring for themselves":** "Love feasts" are thought to be communal meals shared among Christians of a given church, similar to our church potlucks. Jude states that these false teachers are using these occasions for their self-gratification, self-importance, and sensual conduct (2 Peter 2:13). A "hidden reef" refers to a dangerous reef just below the surface of the water; ships striking such a reef will be destroyed, and many lives lost as a result.[115] Such are these men: their true intentions lie just beneath their superficial "Christian" demeanor, waiting to sink yet another inattentive soul.
- **"Clouds without water, carried along by winds":** Clouds that carry water provide rain for crops, therefore contributing to an abundant harvest; these men are like such clouds but are devoid of any benefit (Prov. 25:14). "[C]arried along by winds" implies that they have no moral or spiritual grounding; they not only lie to others, but they themselves are slaves to, and manipulated by, satanic lies.
- **"Autumn trees without fruit, doubly dead, uprooted":** We cannot help but think of the fig tree that Jesus cursed (Mark 11:12–14, 20–21), since it portrayed itself as a fruit-bearing tree when in fact it was barren. Similarly, these "certain men" parade themselves before Christians as being the genuine article but are without "fruit." "Doubly dead" indicates these men were once dead in their sins, then accepted the grace of God, then returned to the world. "Uprooted" indicates a fruit tree that is not only unable to bear fruit

now but will never bear fruit *again*. It is waiting only for the burn pile (John 15:6).
- **"Wild [or, raging] waves of the sea, casting up their own shame like foam"**: These men are restless, untethered, ungrounded, and in a constant state of moral turmoil, because "where jealousy and selfish ambition exist, there is disorder and every evil thing" (James 3:16). Just as waves produce useless foam when they reach the shore, so these men produce nothing but shame (or, have nothing but shameful deeds to give account for) upon reaching the end of their lives and facing their judgment.
- **"Wandering stars, for whom the black darkness has been reserved forever"**: Obviously, actual stars do not wander, but Jude may refer to meteors (which we erroneously call "falling stars" even today), orbiting comets, or planets. The point is: stars are *supposed* to be fixed points of reference in the sky and are so dependable that sailors and other travelers can use them for navigation. But false teachers have no fixed place and are not dependable; instead, they are unstable, untrustworthy, and unwilling to take responsibility for their actions.

The Book of Enoch (1:14–15) is not a biblical book but was (allegedly) written partially by Enoch and then added to by other authors. What makes this quote scriptural, then, is not its source, but its insertion in a writing that *is* worthy of canonicity—i.e., Jude's epistle. Enoch is the one whom God translated into heaven and therefore did not experience physical death (Gen. 5:18–24, Heb. 11:5). It is unclear as to what event or historical age Enoch's prophecy pertains, but Jude offers it as a general statement of divine judgment, not a specific one. Just as the Lord once descended upon the realm of men with "many thousands of His holy ones" to carry out divine justice, so He will again against the entire world (2 Peter 3:7, 10). Jude gives three reasons for such judgment, all related to the "certain men":

- **"to execute judgment upon all [men]"**—God, the Sovereign Authority over the entire universe, has a moral responsibility to defend justice itself, since justice is an inseparable attribute of His divine holiness.

- ❏ "to convict all the ungodly of their ungodly deeds …"—the verb "convict" (in this context) carries the meaning of exposing one's crimes as well as punishing him for them.[116]
- ❏ "and of all the harsh things which ungodly sinners have spoken against Him"—because such men have desecrated God's holy Name, they will be brought before the divine tribunal to face their Judge, the Lord Himself.

Jude finishes his denunciation of false teachers with some final observations. "These are grumblers, finding fault, following after their {own} lusts" (1:16a): we only need to look into the books of *Exodus* (e.g., 17:1–7) and *Numbers* (e.g., 11:1–10) to discover God's strong displeasure toward grumblers, murmurers, and complainers among the Israelites (1 Cor. 10:10).

People grumble and complain when their own expectations (desires, or "lusts") go unfulfilled. Those who grumble against God indirectly accuse Him of wrongdoing; the implication is, "If You [God] had done what I expected, then I would have no reason for complaint!" Yet, false teachers have no reservations toward holding God or His people responsible for any denial of their carnal desires.

The same mouths that spew forth grumblings and complaints also pour out flattering words to those people whom the false teachers wish to manipulate for their own agendas (1:16b). They "speak arrogantly" about their knowledge, accomplishments, or love for the Lord, but it is all just empty talk (1 Cor. 8:1–2, 2 Peter 2:18). Or they lavish Christians with praise, but with wicked ulterior motives. They are, in conclusion, false in every respect: what they say, what they do, why they praise, and who they worship.

Questions

1.) What specific ways ought Christians to "contend earnestly for the faith" (1:3) today?

2.) Many churches today, because it is popular and preferable, will magnify God's love, kindness, and forgiveness. Yet they may be conspicuously silent concerning His condemnation against sin and His wrath toward sinners (1:4–16). What is wrong with this? Will ignoring God's condemnation and wrath make these go away?

3.) Jude draws from two major sources to establish his argument against ungodly men: the OT scriptures and physical nature.

   a. What do these two sources have in common?

   b. What is markedly different about these two sources?

   c. Should we also cite these two sources today for the same reason that Jude cited them?

Lesson Thirteen
Prescription for Godly Living (Jude 1:17–25)

Encouragement and Warning (17–23): Having finished his denunciation of these "certain men" who have "crept in unnoticed" (recall 1:4), Jude now provides a positive message to true believers (the "beloved"). "[R]emember the words that were spoken beforehand by the apostles …" (1:17), a message identical to Peter's (2 Peter 3:2). "Apostles" are those men *appointed* by Jesus Christ for the specific purpose of conveying God's word to His church (Rom. 1:1, 1 Cor. 1:1, 12:28, Gal. 1:1, etc.), and who *proved* their appointment with demonstrations of power (2 Cor. 12:12, Heb. 2:3–4).[117] They do not merely speak *of* Christ; they speak *for* Him. "Remember" means Jude's readers were once taught the truth (apostolic teaching) but now need to *remain steadfast* or stand firm in it (1 Cor. 15:1–2).

One specific apostolic teaching of which Jude reminds his readers is that "mockers" will come against the apostles, Christians in general, God's word, and God Himself (1:18a). What these men *mock* is the fact that—so far—God has not met their defiance of the apostles with direct judgment. Jude does not provide the same detail that Peter does (see 2 Peter 3:3–4), but he does agree with Peter that the church is most certainly in the "last time" or final dispensation of world history (see also Heb. 1:1–2).[118] All that follows this is Christ's return and the Final Judgment.

These "mockers" do not follow the Spirit, but "their own ungodly lusts" (1:18b). Paul had warned of these men (2 Tim. 3:1–9), but now they have begun to infiltrate the churches. "These are the ones who cause divisions" (1:19), sowing seeds of discord within the congregations, pitting their own followers against those who maintain the standard of sound teaching. They are "worldly-minded"[119] and therefore have no respect or appreciation for heavenly truth or spiritual values. Their focus is on this world, whereas a Christian's is beyond this world (Col. 3:1–3). These false men have no fellowship with God and are instead hostile to Him (Rom. 8:6–9).

To resist these false teachers and avoid succumbing to their false teaching, Jude gives these prescriptions (1:20–23):

- "**[Be] building yourselves up on your most holy faith.**" While false teachers work at tearing down and causing divisions, Christians are to work at building *up* and "[being] diligent to preserve the unity of the Spirit in the bond of peace" (Eph. 4:3). "[M]ost holy faith" refers (here) to the common faith shared by all believers.
- "**[Be] praying in the Holy Spirit**"—not *to*, but *in*. Christians offer their prayers *to* God *through* the agency (or intercession) of the Holy Spirit (Rom. 8:26–27), just as we also worship in the Spirit (Phil. 3:3). Paul says that "through Him [Christ] we both have our access in one Spirit to the Father" (Eph. 2:18). Whoever keeps God's commandments and prays in the Spirit will certainly have fellowship with the Father.
- "**Keep yourselves in the love of God**"—while God *always* loves us, and loves us unconditionally, He has a special *kind* of love for those who walk in fellowship with Him. This requires something of those people: we are to love one another (John 13:34–35); we are to keep His commandments (John 14:15, 1 John 2:3); we are to follow His Spirit (Gal. 5:16); we are to "abstain from wickedness" (2 Tim. 2:19); etc. In other words, to remain in God's special *love* for His people, we must *live* like His people.
- "**[Be] waiting anxiously for the mercy of our Lord Jesus Christ to eternal life**"—this can refer to the believer's anticipation for heaven, or specifically for Christ's Second Coming (2 Peter 3:12). In either case, he has an eager longing to realize the promise of his salvation in fact, not merely in faith (1 Peter 1:6–9).
- "**And have mercy on some, who are doubting**"—since God has shown *you* mercy, Jude says, then show mercy to others. Believers should direct this mercy or compassion specifically toward those who are wavering in their faith, no doubt under the influence of the false teaching of "certain men."[120]
- "**[S]ave others, snatching them out of the fire**"—i.e., some weak Christians are so close to falling that urgent and even desperate measures are necessary. Jude's instruction is imperative: believers

must not disregard these souls. They are heading for divine judgment ("the fire") if they fall (Heb. 10:26–31); Christians must do something—and soon, casting aside all niceties, pleasantries, decorum, and discomforts.

- **"[A]nd on some have mercy with fear, hating even the garment polluted by the flesh."** Jude provides the necessary balance: mercy is one thing; losing your *own* soul to "save" someone *else's* is quite another. We are to help, but there are limits to what we can do; we are to show compassion and exert strenuous effort, but our primary responsibility is to save our own soul *first*. We may have to lay down our lives for the brethren (1 John 3:16), but we are *never* to lay down our "souls" for *anyone*. Thus, a healthy "fear" for what is at stake is most important.
- **"[H]ating even the garment …"**—"garment" here is figurative, not literal.[121] One's "garment" is his lifestyle, his behavior, and his public image; this can become "polluted" with sinful conduct, and the Christian is not to embrace or enable this but must "hate" it (Rev. 2:6, for example).

To sum up what Jude has just said: holy faith, earnest prayer, godly love, and eager anticipation for Christ's return are characteristics of the Christian life. This requires, however, that we be concerned for those Christians who are weak in spirit, doubting in faith, and entangled in sin. We must not do this at the expense of our own salvation, but we also must not neglect this out of mere self-protection. Being a responsible Christian is a difficult, inconvenient, and often messy affair; it is not for the half-hearted, timid, or indifferent.

Closing Doxology (1:24–25): A doxology is a short and (in the NT) sometimes spontaneous hymn or expression of praise to God.[122] Jude concludes his brief but potent epistle with one of the lengthier doxologies in the NT (1:24–25). "Now to Him [God]" is a common introduction to such a hymn, deferring all glory, honor, and respect to the One who deserves it the most—He who is higher, greater, and wiser than any created being. What God can do for us with His power, authority, and grace (1:24):

- "[K]eep [or, guard] you from stumbling . . . ." Not "stumbling" means "not sinning," thus, standing firm, sure-footed, and free from falling.[123] This does *not* mean God will *prevent* you from sinning by overriding your own free moral will. Nothing in Scripture supports such an idea. It does mean, however, that God's merciful help, divine grace, and inspired word will keep you on the straight and narrow path—*provided* you avail yourself of these gifts (1 Cor. 10:13, 2 Peter 1:8–11.)
- "[M]ake you stand in the presence of His glory . . . ." We cannot "stand" before God on our own, since: we have already "fallen" from His glory by sinning against Him (Rom. 3:23); we are made unworthy of this honor due to this corruption of our souls; and unless we are made holy *by* God, we are unable to be presented *before* Him. Our "standing" is possible through obedience to the gospel (1 Cor. 15:1–2) and, subsequently, the gracious intercession of Jesus Christ (Rom. 5:1–2).
- "**Blameless**" means faultless, innocent, and without condemnation (due to guilt). It is God, through the blood of Jesus, who makes us blameless upon our having obeyed His gospel and dealt responsibly with our sins (Col. 1:21–22). The false teachers whom Jude has denounced in this epistle are *blameworthy* and justifiably condemned; those who walk in fellowship with God are *blameless* and justified through Christ (Rom. 3:23–24).
- "[W]ith great joy"—because God's providential care of His people is cause for rejoicing (Phil. 4:4). Christians, of all people, are to "greatly rejoice with joy inexpressible" (1 Peter 1:8) because of what He has done, what He does now, and what He promises to do for those who entrust their souls to Him.

Jude has warned his fellow Christians of the dangers of false teachers and how subtly these men can worm their way into unsuspecting churches. Faithful Christians must not be oblivious to these same dangers; they must not think they can protect themselves apart from how *God alone* can safeguard them. To resist false teaching and false teachers requires study, preparation, and a pure heart on the part of those who are under attack. It also requires an earnest appeal for divine providence to do what no man or men can do themselves.

Having addressed what God can *do* for His people, Jude now turns his attention to the majesty and power of God Himself (1:25):

- He is the *only* "God" and "Savior"—there is but one God the Father (1 Cor. 8:4–6, Eph. 4:6)—the sole *owner* of life and salvation. This is something every Christian needs to know, teach, and remember often.
- God's salvation is "through Jesus Christ our Lord"—salvation being impossible *apart* from Him. All salvation comes *from* the Father, but it is the Son who makes this available to *us* who call upon His name for help.
- "[To God] be glory, majesty, dominion, and authority … ." Jude exalts God's virtues and attributes and praises Him for these (as in Rev. 5:11–13). "Glory" refers to the dignity, honor, and praise that God, as a divine being, rightly deserves.[124] "Dominion" comes from a Greek word which means might, strength, and power.[125] "Authority" refers to a legal right to something or the power to act. As the Creator, God has the legal right to make laws, enforce laws, reward law-keepers, and punish lawbreakers, all within the context of His Creation.
- "[B]efore all time and now and forever"—another way of saying, "These attributes of God have and will *always* be so, and He is thus *forever* deserving of praise."
- "Amen"—lit., verily, truly, yes, so be it, or let it be so.[126] God the Father, through Jesus Christ His Son, is our "Yes"—our "Amen"—regarding His promises to keep us and take care of us (2 Cor. 1:20, Rev. 3:14). Whatever God says, and whatever God does, is always "Yes/Amen" to safeguarding our souls, and thus always answers our prayers to that end.

This is a powerful ending to a powerful letter. No doubt the truthfulness, potency, and reassurance encouraged the first recipients of this letter. Likewise, it remains a source of encouragement for Christians today.

Questions

1.) Jude does not merely say, in effect, "Be careful of the dangers that come against the church," but teaches that we be *adequately prepared to identify, confront, and resist* those dangers. Is this still good instruction for us today?

   a. What will be the outcome of a church that *knows* about certain dangers threatening it but does not *prepare* to respond to them?

   b. Is this also true in the following scenarios?

   i. Knowing the dangers against your marriage but not doing what is necessary to protect yourself and your spouse from them?

   ii. Knowing the dangers against your children but not proactively giving them life tools necessary to deal with those dangers?

      iii.   Knowing the dangers against your soul but not putting on the "full armor of God" (Eph. 6:10–18) to protect yourself?

      iv.   Knowing the dangers that face the lost but not saying anything to warn—and possibly save—them from succumbing to them?

2.) Why do you suppose the gospel is not an "every man for himself"-kind of religion?

    a.   What does Jude say that indicates otherwise (1:22–23)?

    b.   Yet, despite what other Christians do (or fail to do), what must be our ultimate concern—and why is this?

3.) Why are doxologies (hymns or expressions of praise to God) important to the Christian faith (1:24–25)? What purpose do they serve? Should we write or speak our own doxologies today?

Sources Used for *1 John, 2 John, 3 John,* and *Jude*

Barclay, William. *The Letters of John and Jude.* Philadelphia: Westminster Press, 1976.

Barnes, Albert. *Barnes' Notes*, vol. 13. Grand Rapids: Baker Book House, no date.

Bruce, F. F. *The Epistles of John.* Grand Rapids: Eerdmans Publishing Co., 1970.

Cogdill, Roy E. The New Testament: Book by Book. Marion, IN: Cogdill Foundation Publications, 1975.

Hester, H. I. *The Heart of the New Testament.* Liberty, MO: Quality Press, 1964.

International Standard Bible Encyclopedia (electronic edition). © 1979 by Wm. B. Eerdmans Publishing Co.; database © 2013 by WORDsearch Corp.

Jamieson, Robert, Andrew R. Fausset, and David Brown. *Jamieson, Fausset, and Brown Commentary: Commentary Critical and Explanatory on the Whole Bible (1871)* (electronic edition). Database © 2012 by WORDsearch Corp.

Lenski, R. C. H. *Commentary on the New Testament: The Interpretation of the Epistles of St. Peter, St. John, and St. Jude.* Peabody, MA: Hendrickson Publishers, 1998.

Pearson, Birger A. *Ancient Gnosticism: Traditions and Literature.* Minneapolis: Fortress Press, 2007.

Plummer, A. "The Epistles of John." *Pulpit Commentary*, vol. 22. Peabody, MA: Hendrickson Publishers, no date.

Robertson, A. T. *Word Pictures in the New Testament*, vol. VI. Grand Rapids: Baker Book House, no date.

Salmond, S. D. F. "The Epistle of Jude." *Pulpit Commentary*, vol. 22. Peabody, MA: Hendrickson Publishers, no date.

Schaff, Philip. *History of the Christian Church*, vol. 1. Grand Rapids: Eerdmans Publishing Co., 1995 (originally © 1910 Charles Scribner's Sons).

Strong, James. *Strong's Talking Greek-Hebrew Dictionary* (electronic edition). Database © WORDsearch Corp. (originally published 1890).

Sychtysz, Chad. *1 & 2 Thessalonians Commentary.* Waynesville, OH: Spiritbuilding Publishers, 2024.

Thayer, Joseph. *Thayer's Greek-English Lexicon* (electronic edition). Database © 2005 WORDsearch Corp.

The Complete Word Study: New Testament (electronic edition). Spiro Zodhiates, ed. © 1991 AMG International, Inc. Database © 2008 WORDsearch Corp.

Woods, Guy N. *A Commentary on the New Testament Epistles of Peter, John and Jude* (vol. 5 in commentary series). Nashville: Gospel Advocate Co., 1979.

Unless otherwise noted, Scripture taken from the
NEW AMERICAN STANDARD BIBLE®
Copyright © 1960, 1962, 1963, 1968, 1971, 1972, 1973, 1975, 1977, 1995
by The Lockman Foundation. Used by permission.

Endnotes

1   "According to Eusebius, the emperor Domitian had banished John from Ephesus (in AD 95) because of his continued witnessing about Jesus. He was released 18 months later by Nerva [the Roman emperor who ruled from AD 96–8]" (Robert Jamieson, Andrew Fausset, and David Brown, *Jamieson, Fausset, and Brown Commentary: Commentary Critical and Explanatory on the Whole Bible (1871)*, electronic edition [database © 2004 by WORDsearch Corp.] on Rev. 1:9; bracketed words are mine).

2   Simon J. Kistemaker, *New Testament Commentary: Exposition of the Epistle of James and the Epistles of John* (Grand Rapids: Baker Book House, 1986), 200.

3   Philip Schaff, *History of the Christian Church*, vol. 1 (Grand Rapids: Eerdmans Publishing Co., 1995), 429.

4   "The evidence … regarding the genuineness, authenticity, and canonicity of the Epistle of First John is abundant, reliable, and entirely satisfactory" (Guy N. Woods, *A Commentary on the New Testament Epistles of Peter, John and Jude* [Nashville: Gospel Advocate Co., 1979], 199).

5   Albert Barnes, *Barnes' Notes*, vol. 13 (Grand Rapids: Baker Book House, no date), 272; Roy E. Cogdill, *The New Testament: Book by Book* (Marion, IN: Cogdill Foundation Publications, 1975), 173; Kistemaker, *Epistles of John*, 195–6.

6   Cogdill, *Book by Book*, 174.

7   Henry More first coined the term "Gnosticism" in the 17th century (Birger A. Pearson, *Ancient Gnosticism: Traditions and Literature* [Minneapolis: Fortress Press, 2007], 9).

8   Ibid., 12. Pearson goes on to explain that "God" is split into two identities: the "super-transcendent supreme God" who is completely removed from the physical world, and the lower deity responsible for creating and governing it. "The Gnostics saw evil as something inherent in the material creation itself" (106). Since the supreme God cannot be responsible for an evil and sinful world, he must therefore be completely

detached from it. The only way men can access him is through mystical knowledge.

9   This list is quoted verbatim from Kistemaker, *Epistles of John*, 212; bracketed words are mine.

10   Adapted from Barclay, *Letters*, 9–11.

11   R. C. H. Lenski, *Commentary on the New Testament: The Interpretation of the Epistles of St. Peter, St. John, and St. Jude* (Peabody, MA: Hendrickson Publishers, 1998), 366.

12   This is referred to as a "neuter relative" rather than a personal pronoun (A. T. Robertson, *Word Pictures in the New Testament*, vol. VI [Grand Rapids: Baker Book House, no date], 204).

13   "The fellowship which Christians have with God relates to the following points: (1) Attachment to the same truths, and the same objects; love for the same principles, and the same beings … (2) The same *kind* of happiness, though not in the same *degree* … (3) Employment, or cooperation with God … (4) We have fellowship with God by direct communion with him, in prayer, in meditation, and in the ordinances of religion … (5) The Christian will have fellowship with his God and Saviour in the triumphs of the latter day, when the scenes of judgment shall occur, and when the Redeemer shall appear, that he may be admired and adored by assembled worlds" (Barnes, *Barnes' Notes*, 281–2).

14   "'These things we are writing,' Zahn rightly says, includes the entire New Testament literature, especially that which was written directly by the apostolic witnesses but also that which is based on their witness, the literature to which John is now contributing this letter and will contribute his Gospel and his Revelation" (Lenski, *Interpretation*, 380).

15   James Strong, *Strong's Talking Greek-Hebrew Dictionary*, electronic edition (database © 2012 by WORDsearch Corp.), G2842.

16   This affirmation—that Jesus *is* the Son of God—defeats any form of Gnosticism which holds that Christ (as a spirit) left Jesus the Man prior to His death upon the cross (as Cerinthus taught). John links the shed blood of Jesus with the shed blood of His Son—they are not two different Beings producing two different bloods, but one. It also refutes

any "phantom-theories" that claim that Jesus was not a real, flesh-and-blood Person. John saw Him in the flesh and is an eyewitness to the blood which poured out of Him (John 19:31–37).

17   "'Cleanseth [so reads the King James Version (KJV)] is from the verb *katharizei* [from which we get the word "catharsis"], in the present tense, thus revealing that it is a constant process, conditioned on our walking in the light. As we thus walk the blood operates to keep us constantly cleansed from the defilement of sin and the condemnation which attends it" (Woods, *New Testament Epistles*, 217; bracketed words are mine).

18   *Strong's* (electronic), G3670.

19   Lenski, *Interpretation*, 393.

20   Joseph Thayer, *Thayer's Greek-English Lexicon*, electronic edition (database © 2005 WORDsearch Corp.), G3875. An advocate is the direct opposite of an accuser; Jesus is called our Advocate in Scripture, whereas Satan is our accuser (Rev. 12:9–10).

21   Adapted from Barclay, *Letters*, 44–5.

22   "St. John knows nothing of such compromises. Love is love, and hate is hate, and between the two there is no neutral ground, any more than between life and death, or between Christ and [an] antichrist" (Plummer, *Pulpit Commentary*, 22; bracketed word is mine).

23   "Stumbling" comes from the Greek word *skandalon*, which refers to a snare, trap, something put into the path of another (to trip him up), and a cause for sin (Mat. 16:23, 18:7, John 16:1, Rom. 14:13, etc.) (Strong, *Dictionary* [electronic], G4625).

24   "The threefold grouping relates to spiritual maturity, not years reckoned by the calendar" (Bruce, *The Epistles of John*, 58). Other commentators see it differently, but this view seems the most natural explanation of this difficult passage.

25   *Strong's* (electronic), G3962.

26   Woods, *New Testament Epistles*, 238.

27   Thayer, *Lexicon* (electronic), G1939. For example, Paul uses the word in Phil. 1:23 and 1 Thess. 2:17 with no reference to anything sinful or forbidden.

28   Strong, *Dictionary* (electronic), G500.

29   "There is a play on words in the Greek Testament here, not observable in the translation. If the false teachers were *anti-christoi* [lit., against (the) Anointed (One)], these to whom John wrote were *christoi*, anointed ones" (Woods, *New Testament Epistles*, 245; bracketed words are mine).

30   The Greek verb *oida* ("to know") refers not to acquired knowledge, but innate or already-known knowledge; thus, not new truths, but a truth they already know (Kistemaker, *Epistle of John*, 279).

31   On the other hand, it is also true that the early church, in lieu of the fully revealed or fully recorded gospel, did rely upon the prophetic testimonies of those endowed with miraculous gifts, including the apostles themselves. Thus, they "all know" *not* because every Christian has miraculous ability, but because some did, and these proved what was truly from God (through His Spirit) and therefore what was not (see 4:1ff).

32   Such was the position of Cerinthus, a late first-century Gnostic who claimed that Jesus (the Man) and Christ (the Divine Being) were two different people, and that, while Jesus did indeed die on the cross, Christ could not have (see "Introduction: Purpose of Writing"). Cerinthus, then, attempted to deny Jesus as the Son of God, yet he claimed to have fellowship with the Father.

33   The word "confidence" (2:28) can also be translated "boldness." "The world 'boldness' (*parresia*), as here used, signifies 'freedom of speech,' the right to speak out as one thinks, and was used by the ancient Greeks of their privilege as free citizens" (Woods, *New Testament Epistles*, 254).

34   The Greek word here (*teknon*) means "child" or "children" (with no respect to gender), or "son(s)," as the context dictates here a reference to an inheritance (Strong, *Dictionary* [electronic], G5043).

35   Barclay, *Letters*, 73; all emphases are his.

36   Lenski, *Interpretation*, 450.

37   "The Greek word for 'see' involves more than a merely physiological occurrence; it means 'perceiving,' 'recognizing,' even 'appreciating'

(Tittmann)" (JFB, *Commentary* [electronic], on 3:2).

38   "John states a fact: 'Everyone who has this hope … purifies himself.' He refrains from expressing a wish ('may purify himself'), a possibility ('he may purify himself'), or a command ('he ought to purify himself'). John puts this stated fact in positive terms. The believer lives in the hope of becoming conformed to Jesus Christ, and the more he contemplates this truth the more he purifies himself of sin" (Kistemaker, *Epistles of John*, 296).

39   "In the Greek text, both *sin* and *lawlessness* have the article before them [thus, "the sin"; "the lawlessness"]; each term is the equivalent of the other and they are, therefore, interchangeable" (Woods, *New Testament Epistles*, 261; bracketed words are mine).

40   "Those who live as the devil lives must be regarded as belonging to the devil; in exhibiting the traits and characteristics of the devil, they evidence the fact that they are his children" (Woods, *New Testament Epistles*, 269).

41   Compare this phrase with that found in Mat. 19:4, 8, 24:21, John 1:1–2, John 9:32, Heb. 1:10, and 2 Peter 3:4. All these uses refer to the same "beginning": the creation of the physical universe and humankind (as depicted in Gen. 1). Here is another thought: "John Albert Bengel wisely replies, '*from the beginning* [means] from the time when the devil is the devil.' How long Satan remained in his pristine angelic state, we do not know. When he fell into sin, he became the originator and instigator of sin" (Kistemaker, *Epistles of John*, 302; bracketed word is his).

42   John mentions Cain without any previous details, as though the entire world knows of him; yet he does not mention Abel by name. "Human nature is the same as of old. There is still a Cain, the world, hating its Abel, the church" (Plummer, *Pulpit Commentary*, 73). Also, "slew" [Greek, *sphazo*] means literally "to cut the throat of," as a sacrificial animal. It is used only here and in *Revelation* (Robertson, *Word Pictures*, 224).

43   Paul comes to this same conclusion, but in different words; Rom. 14:15, 20, and 1 Cor. 8:11–13. Consider also Jesus' words in Mat. 25:45: "Then He will answer them [those who withheld brotherly love—my words], 'Truly I say to you, to the extent that you did not do it to one of

the least of these, you did not do it to Me.'"

44 "We are taught here that he who does not love his brother actually *has no brother to love,* for in his failure to comply with this normal and natural principle [i.e., to love his brother in Christ], he demonstrates that God is not his Father. In refusing to love one of God's family, he simply excludes himself from the family itself!" (Woods, *New Testament Epistles,* 274; bracketed words are mine).

45 JFB, *Commentary* (electronic), on 3:13.

46 "We know" (perfect active indicative in the Greek) means, "We have come to know and still know" (Robertson, *Word Pictures,* 225). John uses this expression frequently, often rhetorically, as in, "We have already learned the lesson and have learned it well." It is like Paul's rhetorical "Or do you not know?" statements (Rom. 6:3, etc.).

47 "Murder is simply hate expressed in an overt act; and when it does not issue in this fashion, it is due to other causes than those which reside in the heart of the hater. If hate does not result in murder, the reason is to be sought, not in the hate, but in the lack of opportunity or means, or courage, of the hater" (Woods, *New Testament Epistles,* 279).

48 "Need" is the operative word here. We must never help someone only to make ourselves feel better, nor can those in need make demands of our help by making us feel guilty, making threats, or by being unchristian themselves in any way. Positive peer pressure (to do the right thing) is permissible, which is what Paul used to motivate the Corinthians (2 Cor. 9:1–5) and is what John is doing in the present passage. But just because someone claims to be "in need" and then tries to obligate Christians to help him does not mean he truly *is* in need. However, in cases where the need cannot be determined as being real or imagined, it would be best to err on the side of helping rather than withholding.

49 A "false prophet" [Greek, *pseudoprophetes*] is not one who is merely ignorant of what he teaches or has not yet learned a better understanding of his material. Apollos, for example, taught a limited and incorrect understanding of Jesus' ministry (Acts 18:24–28); when corrected, he changed his teaching to reflect a better understanding, as provided by Priscilla and Aquila. Prior to this correction, however, he was *not* a false

prophet (or false teacher) since he did not mean to lead anyone astray in his teaching. Likewise, a Christian who has a different *opinion* than others about a religious subject cannot possibly be a false prophet if indeed he expresses his view *as* an opinion. Ignorance and opinions, by themselves, do not make men false prophets. A false prophet/teacher is one who *knowingly* and even *maliciously*—for whatever reason— leads his listeners to believe something that is not true (as described in 2 Peter 2:1–3 and implied in Mat. 7:15–20). Often, he claims to have a privileged or even exclusive revelation from God that allegedly puts him in a superior position to everyone else—including Christ's own apostles. See comments on 2 John 1:7 for a more detailed description of this.

50   "Test" (or "prove") here is from the Greek word *dokimazete* which refers to the testing or assaying of metals. "Put them to the acid test of truth as the metallurgist does his metals. If it stands the test like a coin, it is acceptable (*dokimos*, II Cor. 10:18), otherwise it is rejected (*adokimos*, I Cor. 9:27; II Cor. 13:5–7)" (Robertson, *Word Pictures*, 229). The specific "test" here would be: "Do you believe that Jesus Christ has come in the flesh or not?"

51   Woods, *New Testament Epistles*, 287.

52   We should clarify a statement that John makes here: "everyone who loves is born of God and knows God" (4:7b). Taken alone, it might appear that loving people are in fellowship with God based solely upon the love that they demonstrate to others. This is not true and violates the context not only of this epistle but also the entire NT teaching on "love." Being a loving person is certainly a noble thing; being in fellowship with God requires obedience to His commandments in love. Even wicked people can love (or be loving) when they want to, or in a manner that suits their purposes. What John means, then, is that everyone who loves like God loves must also "know" Him, since no one can produce godly love without first becoming a child of God.

53   "Know" here means personally, intimately, and experientially. In the Greek, it reads, "He who did not come to know God," meaning that not only does such a person *not know* God (presently), but that he has *never* really known God at all (*ibid.*, on 4:8).

54   "The Greek verb tense [of "confess"] implies that this is done once

for all" (JFB, *Commentary* [electronic], on 4:15; bracketed words are mine). "The radical meaning is 'acknowledgment,' 'avowal,' with the implication of a change of conviction or of course of conduct on the part of the subject" (H. E. Jacobs, "Confession," *ISBE* [electronic]). Robertson adds: "This confession of the deity of Jesus Christ implies surrender and obedience also, not mere lip service" (*Word Pictures*, 234).

55   This is the case, even though different words may be used (in the NASB): Acts 4:31, "boldness"; 2 Cor. 3:4, "confidence"; Eph. 3:12, "boldness" and "confidence"; Heb. 3:14, "assurance"; 10:19, "confidence"; 10:22, "full assurance"; 10:35, "confidence"; 11:1, "assurance"; etc.

56   As I understand it, "perfect love" is an ideal objective, as in Mat. 5:48. Our love for God may be ever *nearing* perfection but given the limitations of our earthly humanity we will never be able to achieve it absolutely. As this love increases, however, our fear decreases (John 5:24). Thus, "If it should exist in any soul in an absolutely perfect state, that soul would be entirely free from all dread in regard to the future" (Barnes, *Barnes' Notes*, 334). As it is, no doubt *every Christian* has some reservation (however small) about their presentation before God. On this, recall notes on 3:21.

57   Plummer, *Pulpit Commentary*, 105.

58   Barclay, *Letters*, 104.

59   Note the difference in order between the two passages: in John 19:34, it says "blood and water"; in 1 John 5:6, it says "by water and blood."

60   *NASB Greek-Hebrew Dictionary*, electronic edition (© 1981, 1988 The Lockman Foundation), G3609a.

61   "This is a terrible picture of the Graeco-Roman world of the first century A.D., which is confirmed by Paul in Romans 1 and 2 and by Horace, Seneca, Juvenal, Tacitus" (Robertson, *Word Pictures*, 245). It is no less true today, and no less obvious to those enlightened by God's word to see the world as it really is.

62   The two verbs "know" in 1 John 5:20 are from different Greek words. The first "know" means understanding or perception; the second

means personal or experiential knowledge. It is as if John is saying, "With the understanding you have of the Father (through His Son), you are able to enjoy a personal relationship with Him."

63 JFB, *Commentary* (electronic), on 5:20.

64 Barclay, *Letters*, 127.

65 Bruce, *The Epistles of John*, 134.

66 Robertson, *Word Pictures*, 249.

67 Lenski, *Interpretation*, 550.

68 Woods, *New Testament Epistles*, 332.

69 JFB, *Commentary* (electronic), on 1:1.

70 Cogdill, *Book by Book*, 180.

71 These four are: Gaius of Macedonia, who was dragged into the Ephesian theater along with Paul and Aristarchus during the "no small disturbance" there (Acts 19:29). Gaius of Derbe, who accompanied Paul on the last leg of his third missionary journey (Acts 20:4). Gaius of Corinth, whom Paul personally baptized (1 Cor. 1:14) and who gave Paul room and board while he stayed in that city (Rom. 16:23), assuming these two passages refer to the same man. Gaius, to whom John addresses his third epistle.

72 Kistemaker, *Epistles of John*, 209.

73 The NASB translators have inserted the word "some" in this phrase (" … {some} of your children …"), implying that *other* "children" are *not* walking in truth—which may in fact be the case (as he implies in 1:7–10).

74 JFB, *Commentary* (electronic), on 1:5. While John makes the request to this "lady," the plural pronoun he uses later in the verse ("we") indicates again that he is writing to a group of people, not a literal woman.

75 The word used here is *prago*, lit., "to progress (ahead of); to lead before; to go before" (Strong, *Dictionary* [electronic], G4254). In other words, these deceivers styled themselves as "progressives"; then John warns, "Whoever is (such) a progressive" is in error. This is particularly interesting to us today because many modern, contemporary-styled

"Christian" churches boast about being "progressive," and teach what is beyond the NT pattern. "Modernism, under the guise of progressiveness, is shrewd and adroit in its method of approach. It begins by reminding us that we live in the twentieth century [now, the twenty-first century!—MY WORDS], not the first; that conditions have changed and in our day necessitate a different and modernized approach; that the New Testament was never intended to be a stereotyped arrangement for all succeeding ages; and that 'sanctified common sense' must be utilized in adapting its message to our time" (Woods, *New Testament Epistles*, 348).

76 Robertson, *Word Pictures*, 254.

77 "The Greek verb tense implies that such persons actually do come and are sure to come" (JFB, *Commentary* [electronic], on 1:10).

78 Kistemaker, *Epistles of John*, 383.

79 Strong, *Dictionary* (electronic), G5463.

80 "Do not give him a greeting" here means, in essence, "Do not wish him joy; do not hail, or salute him. The word used expresses the common form of salutation, as when we wish one health, success, prosperity ... It would be understood as a wish for success in the enterprise in which they were embarked; and though we should love all men, and desire their welfare, and sincerely seek their happiness, yet we can properly wish no success in a career of sin and error" (Barnes, *Barnes' Notes*, 366).

81 JFB, *Commentary* (electronic), on 1:12.

82 "The term *children* includes John's friend Gaius and all other Christians who have come to know the truth through the preaching and teaching ministry of the apostle" (Kistemaker, *Epistles of John*, 391).

83 Lenski, *Interpretation*, 581.

84 "Name" is capitalized in the NASB (and a few other versions and translations), but this is a decision of the translators, not the original text. In the original Greek text, *all* the words are capitalized; thus, it is context which determines how these words will be understood in (say) an English translation of them. Other Bible versions say "his name's sake" [KJV], "the sake of the name" [English Standard Version, or ESV],

and "his Name's sake" [New King James Version, or NKJV].

85 Bruce, *The Epistles of John*, 151; bracketed words are mine.

86 Robertson has a good theory, albeit unproved: "[This is not] a reference to II John … , but an allusion to a brief letter of recommendation … sent along with the brethren in verses 5 to 7 or to some itinerant brethren." He goes on to say that while such a letter might have been "brief and a mere introduction," it was nonetheless important and should have been taken seriously by Diotrephes and the rest of his church (*Word Pictures*, 263; bracketed words are mine).

87 "Diotrephes" is a compound name meaning, "nourished by or foster-child of Zeus." This may have been his given name, or it may reveal the pagan culture from which he was converted. John never *says* that Diotrephes is not a Christian, but certainly indicates that he is not *acting* like a Christian, and later (in 1:11) implies that his claim to *be* a Christian may indeed by betrayed by such actions.

88 Paul had a similar problem with some of the proud Corinthians (1 Cor. 4:6–8) and the so-called "most eminent apostles" among them who would not listen to his words (2 Cor. 11:5).

89 Thayer, *Lexicon* (electronic), G5396. Kistemaker translates it "malicious gossip" (*Epistles of John*, 397).

90 Robertson, *Word Pictures*, 264.

91 Barclay, *Letters*, 157.

92 S. D. F. Salmond, "The Epistle of Jude," *Pulpit Commentary*, i.

93 Cogdill, *Book by Book*, 119.

94 Barclay, *Letters*, 178.

95 Woods, *New Testament Epistles*, 373.

96 Lenski, *Interpretation*, 603; bracketed words are mine.

97 Eusebius, one of the most prominent early church historians, questioned Jude's canonicity because few early church fathers quoted it. Thus, *Jude* (along with *2 Peter*) was originally considered *antilegomena* [lit., books that are spoken against], but later all doubts concerning Jude's inspiration, authenticity, and relevance to the church were overcome (JFB, "Jude: Introduction," *Commentary* [electronic]).

98 Robertson, *Word Pictures*, 183.

99 Woods, *New Testament Epistles*, 375.

100 Barnes, *Barnes' Notes*, 381. Lenski proposes: "[W]hen Jude wrote, his brother James was dead (had been killed in Jerusalem at Easter in 66). Jude is stepping in where his brother James might have otherwise done so" (*Interpretation*, 606).

101 Cogdill, *Book by Book*, 119.

102 In the lists of the twelve disciples-turned-apostles, it reads "Judas {the son} of James," the most natural meaning being that he *is* a son and not a brother of James. Translators insert "the son" for this reason, since it is inappropriate for a man to be called "of" his brother; rather, his father is meant. In Matthew and Mark's listing of these men, Judas is not mentioned at all, but Thaddeus is (Mat. 10:2–4, Mark 3:16–19); in Luke's listings (Luke 6:16, Acts 1:13), Thaddeus is not mentioned, but Judas is. The natural answer for this is that Thaddeus is also known as Judas.

103 Strong, G1401; see also G1210.

104 The earliest manuscripts read "beloved"; later manuscripts read "sanctified"; both words refer to the same group of people, who are both beloved *and* sanctified by God (JFB, *Commentary* [electronic], on 1:1).

105 Strong, *Dictionary* (electronic), G2839.

106 Jesus used a form of the same Greek word when teaching that we must "strive" to enter the kingdom (Luke 13:24); similarly, Paul told Timothy to "Fight the good fight of faith" (1 Tim. 6:12).

107 JFB, *Commentary* (electronic), on 1:3. Cogdill adds: "[I]n Jude 3 we have a prefix added to this term, 'agonize,' which increases the intensity of the word and makes it more emphatic, and therefore, lays upon the Christian greater obligation" (*Book by Book*, 119).

108 "The Greek (*pareisduein*) is a very expressive word. It is used of the spacious and seductive words of a clever pleader seeping gradually into the minds of a judge and jury; it is used of an outlaw slipping secretly back into the country from which he has been expelled; it is used of the slow and subtle entry of innovations into the life of state, which in the end undermine and break down ancestral laws. It always indicates

a stealthy insinuation of something evil into a society or situation" (Barclay, *Letters*, 179).

109 Lenski believes Peter's letter (*2 Peter*) was predictive in nature ("This will happen"), while Jude's letter is conclusive in nature ("This has happened"). "Jude's readers still have Peter's letter. Jude points them to Peter's own prophecy which had been made to them a few years ago; what Peter prophesied has now come to pass. The enemy has arrived, the readers must contend earnestly" (*Interpretation*, 612).

110 The word "domain" is from the Greek word *arche*, which most often in Scripture means a "beginning," "origin," or "the first thing in a series" (think of "archetype"). It can also have the meaning, as in the present context, of an estate, domain, principality, or habitation (Thayer, *Lexicon* [electronic], G746).

111 Some claim that because Satan and his angels (demons) are free to conduct their business of waging war against Christians (Eph. 6:12, Rev. 12:17), they must not be under "eternal bonds." Yet, this assumes "bonds" to be literal in clearly spiritual context. Satan, for example, is said to have been "bound" with a "great chain" for a "thousand years" in an "abyss" (Rev. 20:1–3), but such language only communicates a certain action (the long but finite curtailing of Satan's power and jurisdiction), not literal things or measurements. It is entirely reasonable to conclude that the "bonds" of these angels to whom Jude refers are not literal restraints, but also refer to a restraining of their former power and activity. In other words, whatever business they once conducted for the Lord, they are no longer privileged to participate in it.

112 To clarify, an "angel" is a generic term for an otherworldly, non-human, and non-divine being. There are angels of God, to be sure, but there are also angels of Satan (see Mat. 26:41). Just as there are levels of authority among God's angels, it is reasonable to assume that this is true for Satan's angels as well, Satan himself being the highest-ranking of the fallen angels.

113 "Strange flesh" necessarily implies "horrible licentiousness, not simply with women not their wives or in other nations, but even unnatural uses (Rom. 1:27) for which the very word 'sodomy' is used (Gen. 19:4–11)" (Robertson, *Word Pictures*, 189).

114 "Dreaming" can also mean making a hasty commitment or vow to God that you have not really thought through, or have no real plan to keep, as in Eccles. 5:1–7. Such people "do not know they are doing evil" (Eccles. 5:1). However, the context of Jude 1:8 indicates men who *do* know what they are saying, but do not care whether it is true, but simply want to gratify their own desires.

115 *Spilas* means "hidden reefs"; *spilo* means "stain, blemish, defect, or disgrace" (Strong, *Dictionary* [electronic], G4694 and G4696, respectively). There is apparently some disagreement over which word Jude intended to use, or did use, in this verse. Thus, some believe "hidden reefs" should instead refer to some kind of spoilage or corruption that these "certain men" bring into the otherwise upright gathering of Christians, citing 2 Peter 2:13 for corroboration. In fact, both Greek words (and their meanings) apply equally to the situation Jude describes.

116 Thayer, *Lexicon* (electronic), G1651.

117 Woods wisely notes: "Had Jude been an apostle, as some affirm, it is reasonable to suppose that he would have [here] adduced his apostolic authority … [As it is,] the statement is such as would have been made by one not an apostle" (*New Testament Epistles*, 402; bracketed words are mine).

118 "It was a Hebrew idea that time was divided into two great periods—'this age' and 'the age to come,' which were parted by the coming of Messiah. The 'age to come,' or the Messianic age, was in principle introduced by Messiah's first advent [coming or appearance—MY WORDS], but it was to be finally brought in by his second advent …" (Salmond, *Pulpit Commentary*, 13–14).

119 "Worldly-minded" means natural (in their thinking); lit., psychical [Greek, *psuchikos*], as pertaining to unspiritual earthly life (Thayer, *Lexicon* [electronic], G5591). "The Spirit of God was not in the lives or the thoughts of these men, and hence they were creators of division, and sensual. Their pretension was that they were the eminently spiritual. But in refusing the Divine Spirit they had sunk to the level of an animal life, amoral in itself, and productive of confusion to the Church" (Salmond, *Pulpit Commentary*, 14).

120 "This reading ["have mercy on some …"] is supported by all the earliest manuscripts. But several other early manuscripts read, 'And reprove [or, correct] those who are doubting.' The two words look very similar in Greek: *eleate* ('have pity') and *elegchete* ('reprove'); they could have easily been confused one for the other. The idea seems to be that saints are to have pity on or reprove those who have been affected by the false teachings and are now wavering between truth and falsehood. They need to be rescued" (JFB, *Commentary* [electronic], on 1:22; bracketed words are mine).

121 Barnes says that this may be an allusion to the garment by one who suffered from plague, or the clothing of the dead, which, under the Law, would render the living unclean if touched (Num. 19:11), or the garments of those who were contaminated with leprosy (*Barnes' Notes*, 403). I believe him to be correct in this understanding, though Jude uses "garment" in more of a figurative sense than a literal one, as I explain in my exposition of this passage.

122 Examples of this can be found in Rom. 11:33–36, 16:25–27, Eph. 3:20–21, Phil. 4:20, Heb. 13:20–21, 1 Peter 4:11b, and 5:11.

123 Strong, *Dictionary* and Thayer, *Lexicon* (both electronic), G679.

124 Strong, *Dictionary* (electronic), G1391.

125 *Ibid.*, G2904.

126 Thayer, *Lexicon* (electronic), G281.

www.ingramcontent.com/pod-product-compliance
Lightning Source LLC
Chambersburg PA
CBHW050819090426
42737CB00021B/3436